SECRET
SPITFIRES

SECRET SPITFIRES

BRITAIN'S HIDDEN CIVILIAN ARMY

HOWMAN & CETINTAS with GAVIN CLARKE

The History Press

First published 2020
This paperback edition first published 2022

The History Press
97 St George's Place, Cheltenham,
Gloucestershire, GL50 3QB
www.thehistorypress.co.uk

British Library Cataloguing in Publication Data.
A catalogue record for this book is available from the British Library.

ISBN 978 1 80399 037 8

Typesetting and origination by The History Press
Printed and bound in Great Britain by TJ Books Limited, Padstow, Cornwall.

Trees for LYfe

CONTENTS

Foreword by Maggie Appleton MBE, CEO RAF Museum 7
Foreword by Maj. Gen. (ret.) Frederick F. Roggero USAF 9
High Flight 11

Introduction: Building a Legend 13
    John Gillespie Magee Jr: A Remarkable Life 25
    The Engineering and Design that Made the Spitfire Special 28

Chapter 1: The Road to Dispersal 31
    Spitfire Supply Lines Uncovered 48
    Race and Reaction: Birth of the Spitfire 50
    We Saw it Burn: Testimony from Inside the Firestorm 53
    Secret Saviour of the Spitfire 58

Chapter 2: People and Places of the Secret Factories 60
    By the Numbers: Secret Factories' Facts and Figures 78
    A Walk Through Supermarine's Hidden Design HQ 88
    How to Hide a Workforce 94
    This Island Salisbury: War Comes to the City 96

Chapter 3: Day in the Life of a Factory 103
    Beatrice Shilling: The Woman who Saved the Spitfire 124
    Careless Talk Costs Lives 126
    From Prototype to Production 131
    Uncle Sam's Rolls-Royce Engines 133

Chapter 4: Take it Away: Test Pilots, Danger and the ATA   135
    Life on the Edge: The Test Pilots' Story   150
    One Idea, 24 Marques: Welcome to the Versatile Spitfire   155
    Spitefuls and Seafires   159
    The Spitfire in Pieces   161

Chapter 5: Clocking Off: Life Outside the Factory Shift   166
    Not Just Digging for Victory   188
    Salisbury's Stars and Stripes Hospital   194
    Radio Days that Shaped a Nation   198

The People of Secret Spitfires   202

Norman Parker: From Barnardo's Boy to Spitfire Historian   210
Secret Spitfires' Next Chapter   215
About the Authors   217
Credits and Contributors   218
Notes   220

FOREWORD

MAGGIE APPLETON MBE, CEO RAF MUSEUM

It's a real privilege to be asked to contribute to a book that reveals the incredible story of the Secret Spitfires. When the documentary team shared their vision with me some years ago of uncovering the lost history of Spitfire production during the war, it was clear they had discovered a real gem of a tale – something that needed to be polished and placed on full public display for the world to appreciate.

The narrative uncovered in this book aligns beautifully with the RAF Museum's mission to inspire everyone with the RAF story – the people who shape it and its place in our lives. *Secret Spitfires* is a story of British character, determination, bravado, joy and pain. It is a story of ordinary people – the majority of them women – standing up, very quietly and modestly, to the forces of Hitler that had bombed Southampton's major Spitfire works in the mistaken belief that destroying them would diminish the threat posed by the Royal Air Force. The thrill and sheer impertinence of these dispersed Spitfire factories, 'hidden' in plain sight, was clearly a story begging to be told.

Around 10,000 Spitfires were built covertly across a network of garages, bus depots, outbuildings, garden sheds, even in spare bedrooms, making a critical difference to the war effort. And at a time when nothing can escape the social media spotlight and every voice clamours to be heard, it is remarkable that, until very recently, these women and men remained silent about their extraordinary contribution.

Once given the opportunity to reveal their stories, however, the most amazing characters have shone through. Their testaments bring to life teams of individuals who played their part in the manufacture of components for this most iconic of aircraft. They had only limited knowledge of the scope of their enterprise and yet continued to work with a clear and steadfast pride and faith that somehow makes this story even more meaningful and significant.

Secrets sometimes need to be told. This is one of those times.

FOREWORD

MAJ. GEN. (RET.) FREDERICK F. ROGGERO
USAF CHAIRMAN, ROYAL AIR FORCE
MUSEUM AMERICAN FOUNDATION

In our twenty-four-hour media age it is debatable whether a story could ever remain secret, let alone for 70 years. It is therefore not surprising that the producers of the film *Secret Spitfires* greeted the discovery of the story of covert production of Spitfires during the Second World War with a degree of scepticism. How could the manufacture of one of the most iconic aircraft ever produced have occurred behind nondescript facades in southern England, particularly in a small rural city such as Salisbury? But this is exactly what happened and the research unfolds amazing stories of Spitfires being built in secret, mainly by women. You didn't talk about such things during the war and, even now, it took all powers of persuasion to extract the fascinating stories from the women who worked on those production lines.

With thousands of men away serving in the armed forces, British women played a vital role by not only running their households, managing a daily battle of rationing, recycling and growing produce but also by answering the call to become mechanics, bus drivers, engineers and munitions workers. This story not only reveals how these women found themselves on a factory line, but also how the filmmakers' investigations peeled away the layers of secrecy that surrounded their war work. The result was an exposure of an amazing tale initially told in the film. However, the amount of research and hours of interviews extracted from these pioneering women was too much for one film so this book tells for the first time their incredible stories in full.

By 1944 up to half a million American servicemen were based in Britain working with the RAF to take on the Third Reich in the air and on the ground. More than 200 airfields were occupied or newly built by the United States Army Air Force (USAAF), with each one housing around 2,500 men – many times the population of nearby villages. Secret Spitfires highlights the very positive effect their presence had on the morale of the hard-pressed British. It reflects on the huge impact they had on British life and how they changed the places they inhabited, not least Salisbury. On their departure, they left behind them an enduring legacy and fond memories for those they met.

As Chairman of the RAF Museum American Foundation and a Trustee of the Foundation of the National Museum of the United States Air Force, it was my honour to help facilitate the North American premiere of the film Secret Spitfires in the museum's IMAX cinema in 2019. On a wet and windy night, just a few days before the seventy-fifth anniversary of D-Day, approximately 240 residents of Dayton, Ohio – the birthplace of modern aviation – learned how a secret army of mostly women significantly contributed to the vital war work of the Allies by ensuring that Spitfires were ready to fly and fight in defence of freedom.

HIGH FLIGHT

Oh! I have slipped the surly bonds of Earth
And danced the skies on laughter-silvered wings;
Sunward I've climbed and joined the tumbling mirth of sun-split clouds,
– and done a hundred things
You have not dreamed of – wheeled and soared and swung
High in the sunlit silence. Hov'ring there,
I've chased the shouting wind along, and flung
My eager craft through footless falls of air ...
Up, up the long, delirious, burning blue
I've topped the wind-swept heights with easy grace
Where never lark, nor e'er eagle flew –
And, while with silent lifting mind I've trod
The high, untrespassed sanctity of space,
Put out my hand and touched the face of God.

Pilot Officer John Gillespie Magee Jr, 3 September 1941

INTRODUCTION

BUILDING A LEGEND

Soldiers, sailors and airmen through the centuries have taken up arms and – while it's not uncommon to give your gun a name, call your ship a 'she' or paint a face on the nose of your bomber – few have been sufficiently inspired to dedicate a poem to the weapon under their control. Until, that is, Pilot Officer John Gillespie Magee Jr put pen to paper in the summer of 1941.

A young American with film-star good looks, Magee was on course to study at the prestigious Yale University on a scholarship but pulled out to answer the call of duty by enlisting with the Royal Canadian Air Force (RCAF) before his own country had entered the Second World War. Magee would become the first to immortalise the Vickers Supermarine Spitfire in verse; and he did so in a letter home to his parents. That piece he titled 'High Flight' and from the opening two lines it clearly cuts straight to the marriage of form and power that lies in the Spitfire's heart.

'Oh, I have slipped the surly bonds of earth and danced the skies on laughter-silvered wings,' Magee opened.

This young pilot claimed to have begun composing 'High Flight' at 30,000ft (9,144m) in the skies above South Wales, where he'd been stationed for training and where he received his first taste of this new machine. You don't need to be a great student of poetry to hear in Magee's writing his admiration for the transformative blend of design and engineering that, just forty years after the first powered flight, saw humankind at one with the air. Decades on, love for – and interest in – this aircraft has not diminished. It's grown.

The Spitfire was the vision of talented aeronautical engineer Reginald Joseph Mitchell, who led a brilliant team of designers and engineers at seaplane manufacturer Supermarine to deliver this ground-breaking aircraft, just in time for the Second World War. The Spitfire was Mitchell's answer to the Government's call for a new type of mono-winged fighter aircraft to meet the growing threat posed by a rearmed Germany during the 1930s. It quickly established a reputation in the early years of the war, in particular during the Battle of Britain, which was immortalised as a metaphor for plucky survival against seemingly overwhelming odds. In this pivotal conflict, the RAF was in a backs-against-the-wall fight for the future of the homeland against the numerically superior forces of Nazi Germany's air force, the Luftwaffe. Victory was vital, as defeat would have laid Great Britain open to invasion by the German army, which – fresh from the conquest of mainland Europe – was poised on the other side of the English Channel. Yet the RAF prevailed, and the glory of that battle reflected well on the Spitfire.

Contrary to what many will think they know about the Battle of Britain, however, Mitchell's modern combat aircraft was not the most successful in terms of German aircraft shot down. Nor did the Spitfire dominate British squadrons: the RAF's front ranks were dominated by the Hawker Hurricane and the pilots of the Hurricane outperformed those of the Spitfire. During the Battle of Britain, the RAF operated twenty-nine squadrons of Hurricanes versus nineteen of Spitfires, with the pilots of these fighters scoring a total of 656 and 529 kills respectively during the Battle. And yet it's the Spitfire that is most associated with that conflict. Before the war, too, the Hurricane had pipped the Spitfire – this time making it into production first and becoming the RAF's first mono-wing fighter aircraft.

Why then does history and national culture celebrate and revere the Spitfire and not the Hurricane? Unlike the Hurricane, the Spitfire was rooted in an earlier generation of award-winning racing planes also from Mitchell. A combination of streamlined design, use of all-metal body and a powerful Rolls-Royce engine by Mitchell paid dividends in terms of agility, stability and performance and weight. In April 1944 a Spitfire using a new-generation Rolls-Royce engine achieved a record test flight speed in a dive of 606mph (975.26kph) – just over Mach 0.8 – meaning that the Spitfire was on the road to breaking the sound barrier and entering the realm of jet-powered planes. This design and build gave Spitfire pilots a critical edge in their life-or-death fight against the best of the Luftwaffe. Little wonder, then, that the legend of the Spitfire should begin to be fostered in the place that mattered most: among the ranks of the RAF.

Wing Commander Roland Robert Stanford Tuck was one of the first RAF pilots to embrace Mitchell's marvel. Flying a combination of Spitfires and Hurricanes, Tuck would become one of the RAF's top-scoring fighter aces, seeing combat over the beaches of Dunkirk and in the Battle of Britain and claiming more than twenty-seven enemy aircraft before being shot down in January 1942. An experienced pilot flying Gloster Gauntlets and Gladiator biplanes before converting to the new plane, he found the Spitfire a major step change. Based on his not inconsiderable experience, Tuck branded the Spitfire 'an aeroplane beyond all compare'.[1] Such was its impression, Tuck reckoned years later that he could still find his way around the Spitfire cockpit with his eyes closed.

To fly the Spitfire was to slip the 'surly bonds' of earth.

Roaring to go: Spitfire of the Battle of Britain Memorial Flight.

Others echoed Tuck. Richard Hillary was an Australian pilot serving with the RAF's 603 Squadron and assigned to the new machine. Recuperating from wounds following one particular dramatic engagement, Hillary took the time to recount his experiences in the Battle of Britain by writing his memoirs, *The Last Enemy*, published in 1942. It's clear this young pilot was smitten by Mitchell's creation. In his introduction he writes:

> The Spitfires stood in two lines outside 'A' Flight Pilots' room. The dull grey-brown of the camouflage could not conceal the clear-cut beauty, the wicked simplicity of their lines. I hooked up my parachute and climbed awkwardly into the low cockpit. I noticed how small was my field of vision. Kilmartin swung himself onto a wing and started to run through the instruments. I was conscious of his voice, but heard nothing of what he said. I was to fly a Spitfire. It was what I had most wanted to do through all the long dreary months of training. If I could fly a Spitfire, it would be worth it.[2]

Geoffrey Wellum was the youngest RAF pilot to serve in the Battle of Britain. He recalled fondly the union of power and control in the Spitfire during a 2001 interview with historian and author James Holland:

> Bloody thing flew me! You didn't get in, you strapped it to you. A Spitfire could almost think what you wanted to do and it did it. And you didn't think anything about it. It could only respond to what you wanted it to. The Spitfire did that. It responded to anything you wanted to do.[3]

Those who duelled with the likes of Wellum in his Spitfire admitted a certain admiration for this foe. Adolf Galland was a decorated Luftwaffe pilot rising up the ranks in the war's early years. By the time he encountered Spitfires, Galland had gained sufficient experience at the controls of a range of German fighters and had tangled with pilots of enough nations and their machines to recognise a worthy adversary. Galland had served with Hitler's forces during the Spanish Civil War as part of the Condor Legion on the side of Fascist General Franco against the Republicans, and fought during the Nazi invasions of Poland in 1939 and France in 1940. Galland wasn't simply a flyer; he was a tactician, too, and helped formulate the Luftwaffe's battle tactics. If anybody serving with the Luftwaffe was familiar with the nuances and demands of aerial combat in a range of theatres versus a multitude of enemy pilots and planes, it was Galland.

Flushed with the successes of Poland and France but with the Battle of Britain going against them, a frustrated German High Command blamed its pilots rather than the tactics. The veteran commander Galland was flying the Luftwaffe's leading combat aircraft by the time of the Battle of Britain – the lethal Messerschmitt Bf 109 from the formidable German aircraft designer and manufacturer Willy Messerschmitt. It was during one heated confrontation with Luftwaffe commander Herman Göring that Galland apparently conceded his admiration for the RAF's latest fighter. During a meeting with Galland and his fellow officers, Göring had asked what it was they wanted for their squadrons. 'I did not hesitate long,' Galland recalls in his memoirs, *The First and the Last*. 'I should like an outfit of Spitfires for my group.' Galland claims to have been shocked at his outburst and professes to have fundamentally preferred the Luftwaffe's Messerschmitt Bf 109. Galland's quote has been hotly analysed since, but the damage was done. Galland recalls his boss 'stamped off, growling as he went'.[4]

Success for the RAF in the Battle of Britain was a watershed moment in the course of the war. Blocked in the west, Hitler turned his attention to conquest of the east with the invasion of Russia the following year. Nobody could have known at that time, but armed with its dynamic new fighter, the young pilots of the RAF had saved Britain and while the war was far from over, the immediate risk of invasion and conquest of the homeland had passed. The fate of millions had hung on the fortunes of a few hundred in their magnificent new machines and as that battle had raged overhead Prime Minister Winston Churchill encapsulated the spirit of those months in his now famous speech of August 1940. 'Never in the field of human conflict was so much owed by so many to so few,'[5] Churchill told MPs and the nation.

The story of the war is, however, studded with famous weapons from all sides that found their moments, but the Spitfire succeeded where these others failed to become as embedded in the national consciousness and the cultural mainstream. The emotional connection between Spitfire and nation was tangible. People watched the skies above London and the South-East in late summer 1940 and witnessed the aerial battle unfold, craning to see first-hand the Spitfire in action. But how to account for the national passion among those without that front-row seat?

Engagement was key, and campaigns such as Spitfire Funds, a scheme that enabled people to compete in raising money to 'buy' a Spitfire, helped. The idea of sponsoring weapons such as aircraft pre-dated the Second World War but peaked with the Spitfire. The energetic Max Aitken, 1st Baron Beaverbrook, is credited with creating this particular scheme. Appointed Minister of Aircraft Production by Churchill in 1940, press-baron Lord Beaverbrook was the author of different public appeals through his newspapers, which included asking the housewives of Britain in July 1940 to donate their aluminium pots and pans to be melted down for Spitfires, Hurricanes, Blenheims and Wellingtons. The Ministry of

Aircraft Production (MAP) had already begun receiving voluntary donations to pay for the construction of aircraft – Spitfire Funds were a way of formalising that and encouraging contributions. MAP priced the Spitfire at £5,000, although the actual price was far higher, and while you could also 'buy' other aircraft, a stream of favourable news coverage and the power of Beaverbrook's press machine helped ensure it was the Spitfire people wanted. Competition to 'own' a Spitfire became intense, with funds created by councils, businesses, local newspapers and voluntary organisations, with children handing over pocket money and retirees surrendering their pensions. Such was the Spitfire's fame that money rolled in from across the nation, the Commonwealth and beyond: the Nizam of Hyderabad in India donated enough for 152 Squadron to be named in his city's honour.

Filmmakers recognised a good story when they saw one and within a year of Churchill's Battle of Britain speech the cinematic journey that brought the Spitfire story alive for decades following the war had begun. Laying the foundations was General Film Distributors (GFD), which would become J. Arthur Rank Film and then Rank Film Distributors, known to audiences for its muscular gong man in the pre-credits sequence of its films throughout the post-war years. GFD would take Churchill's phrase and serve it back to British audiences in black and white with a reworking of the story behind the Spitfire titled *The First of the Few*, starring Leslie Howard as Mitchell and David Niven as a pilot who embodies the spirit of the RAF men whose names are forever associated with the Spitfire. It's a dramatised account of the Spitfire's creation, from desperate arms race against the Germans with the Messerschmitt, through to first fight. A year after the film was rolled out to British audiences, US cinemas released the film simply as *Spitfire*.

Celluloid wizards rekindled the public's love affair for Spitfire a decade later with the biographical film of boys-own hero Douglas Bader in *Reach for the Sky*. Actor Kenneth More played pipe-smoking Bader, who'd lost both legs in a flying accident but beat the odds to fight during the Battle of Britain and who ended the war as a prisoner. Bader's aerial steed? A Spitfire. The aircraft would hit big screens in full colour with 1969's *Battle of Britain*, with an all-star cast of up-and-coming theatrical blood and old hands, combining documentary style with carefully choreographed air-combat employing aircraft from the era. Years later, it was a Spitfire pilot's timeline that helped tell the desperate story of Dunkirk in Christopher Nolan's critically acclaimed 2017 film. Nolan's first history film saw Tom Hardy's Spitfire pilot engaged in a dogfight over the besieged beaches as desperate British and French soldiers below sought means of escape. The film succeeded in opening a lively debate on the Spitfire's capabilities, specifically whether it would have been possible for a pilot to glide without power and fire the aeroplane's machine guns as portrayed in the film.

Decades on from the Battle of Britain, and not far from where Pilot Officer John Gillespie Magee Jr would eventually be based flying Spitfires at the former RAF Wellingore, Lincolnshire, a new generation of pilots are stewarding the Spitfire's legend. The Battle of Britain Memorial Flight (BBMF) is stationed at RAF Coningsby in Lincolnshire and operates six Spitfires, along with a small selection of other vintage aircraft from the Second World War, wowing crowds at flybys, royal events and public displays. Wing Commander Justin 'Hells' Helliwell, formerly a member of the Memorial Flight, is quick to recognise what made the Spitfire truly stand out. Helliwell was born and raised in a world dominated by the superior speed of the jet engine. He has served in modern, computer-aided combat craft capable of pinpoint precision and deadly accuracy, in aircraft capable of allowing a pilot to engage the enemy without seeing them – a far cry from the close-quarters combat and spiralling turns that defined the Battle of Britain. And yet, despite these advances and refinements, Helliwell feels a direct connection to his predecessors:

> As a fighter pilot, the first time you fly one, you understand what the pilots of old were talking about. I flew a Mk XVI as my first Spitfire, and the moment I rolled her, I knew what they meant. The centre of gravity – it's just pitch perfect so you can almost fly her with a finger and thumb, which is beautiful from a pilot's point of view but as a fighter pilot I knew that was very, very important from an air-to-air combat perspective.

That the Spitfire should perform so impressively in the hands of pilots is a testament to its design and construction. This successful combination would make it a hit with the RAF and ensure continued orders for the maker, Supermarine. More than 22,000 were eventually built, making the Spitfire the fifth most produced aircraft of the Second World War. It came, too, in a staggering twenty-four variations and served in every theatre of war – Europe, North Africa and Asia.

Squadron Leader and former BBMF commander Andy 'Milli' Millikin highlights the importance of a design that made the Spitfire so versatile and successful:

> Arguably it [the Spitfire] was one of the aeroplanes that turned the tide of the war and was extremely important during the Battle of Britain, but also – of course – an aeroplane that continued to be developed and improved. As the tech race started between us and the Germans, new modifications, weaponry and engines came out all the time and the Spitfire was constantly being updated to make sure it was at the cutting edge of technology. The rate at which the aircraft was expanded and improved was absolutely astonishing.

Top to bottom: A new generation maintains the legacy of Supermarine's secret Spitfire army; Squadron Leader and former Battle of Britain Memorial Flight commander Andy "Milli" Millikin: the Spitfire was one of the aeroplanes that turned the tide of the war; Pitch-perfect balance means you can almost fly a Spitfire with a finger and thumb, according to Wing Commander Justin 'Hells' Helliwell, formerly with BBMF.

But there is a story behind this legend – one that receives a good deal less attention. It is the story of how a secret army of civilians was mustered by the Government and Supermarine to help deliver the fighter that was revered then and is loved now, generations later. Just as the Spitfire played an integral role in the shaping of the Second World War, so this secret civilian army would play a crucial role in its delivery, building around 12,000 of the overall total. And they did so, too, not in giant industrial plants as you might expect, but in a network of secret factories tucked away in unassuming and everyday locations across the south of England.

The members of the secret army serving in these factories? As you would expect, boys too young to fight, men of retired age and women – but more women than you'd find almost anywhere in Britain's wartime economy. Women had been mobilised en masse by a Government faced with the need for maximum industrial output to meet the demands of a wartime economy but challenged by the fact that men who'd normally fulfil demand and who'd dominated the industrial workforce had been called up. A pre-war labour surplus had been turned overnight into a shortage, and while the popular perception is of women working in munitions factories, aircraft manufacturing was insatiable in its demands. By 1943[6] women would make up 40 per cent of that sector's workforce, second only to ordnance. Spitfire production specifically, however, saw even greater numbers. No records exist of how many worked in each secret factory but, on average, women broke through the national figure, comprising around 65 per cent of the workforce.

What accounted for this especially high figure? Necessity. The need for an instant workforce to quickly pick up Spitfire production following a dramatic and unique dispersal of manufacturing operations. Yes, the role of women reflected the national picture for a large numbers of workers, but complicating the Spitfire's story was the fact that the factories had not been placed in the typical industrial locations where a ready supply of workers might be found. These factories had been deliberately moved to locations outside major cities to maintain secrecy and that made finding new workers more of a challenge. The women of this workforce therefore lived locally, having laboured in non-technical occupations such as hairdressing and retail, or served in unskilled domestic posts for the officer class or local gentry.

Building the Spitfire was no mean feat for these novices. Not only were these women thrown into the deep end of a new working experience but they were expected to quickly master the tools and techniques required to deliver this advanced fighter – and do so on a vast scale. This secret civilian army built, assembled, fitted and finished thousands upon thousands of fuselages and wings using new and demanding processes never before employed on such a scale in any one factory – never mind in many widely dispersed smaller units.

The names of funds who'd raised money for Spitfires would be painted on fuselages.

These industrial innocents were assigned to environments full of deafening noise, working twelve-hour shifts day and night, handling heavy machinery and engaged in repetitive tasks. They did so, too, with the added stresses and strains of living during wartime – facing the privations of conflict and living under the constant threat of bombing. Their novice status did, however, confer a considerable advantage: they came unencumbered by the baggage of the 'old ways' and found it easier to adapt to the demands placed on Supermarine to deliver Mitchell's new fighter. Starting from scratch, these new recruits would quickly learn the ropes and take on ever-more skilled roles to advance up the ranks as team leaders. They embraced the work and the opportunity to get a crack at what, until then, had been a role dominated by men.

What this unique class of worker might have lacked in experience they made up for in potential and determination. They would exceed the wartime challenge laid before them and defy society's expectations. Driven by a new-found spirit in their venture, the workers of the secret Spitfire factories would deliver the first Spitfire – a Mk 1A, No. R7252 – just six months after Supermarine had been bombed out and sent its operations underground, beginning again more or less from scratch. What followed that first Spitfire in March 1941 was a fleet of thousands.

Clockwise from left: Women comprised
the majority of Supermarine's secret civilian
army; The women were actively recruited to
join Supermarine's secret Spitfire factories;
Airframe Assemblies' Chris Michelle:
the Spitfire lent itself to the small-scale
production of Supermarine's secret factories.

It was a symbiotic relationship. Yes, Mitchell designed the Spitfire and gave the RAF its edge against a tough enemy. But his creation would have been just half the legend it has become had it not been for this unique and hidden workforce. The efforts of these workers helped guarantee the Spitfire's status as the saviour of a nation. Helliwell muses:

> Why did we do so well in the Battle of Britain and beyond? That generation was defending the homeland and the freedoms we enjoy today. So I'm guessing that those boys who were flying – and girls and boys who were supporting them – just put that little bit of extra effort and emotion into what they were doing, whether that was on the ground refuelling them, repairing them, or building them.

To fly the Spitfire was – and is – to become at one with it, and it's easy to understand how new RAF pilots such as Magee and experienced veterans like Tuck approached this legend with a combination of awe, trepidation and relish. Understandable, too, how even the enemy admitted a grudging respect for its nemesis. But while the front-line history of the Spitfire's success is well recorded, less familiar is the inside story of the manufacturing miracle that produced around half of those aeroplanes, founded on the work of a civilian army that toiled around the clock in hidden locations, turning Mitchell's evolving designs into reality. Without them – and without Supermarine's secret factories – this iconic fighter could never have achieved its dramatic or lasting impact.

This is that story.

JOHN GILLESPIE MAGEE JR: A REMARKABLE LIFE

The Spitfire might have been British designed and built, but it was a teenage pilot from America whose poetic masterpiece helped put R.J. Mitchell's aeroplane on the path to celebrity. John Gillespie Magee Jr was a 19-year-old serving with the Royal Canadian Airforce (RCAF) who, like so many other young Allied pilots during the war, would be captivated by the Spitfire. But, while his peers would record their feelings through memoirs, John went further, capturing the transcendental experience of flight itself realised in a Spitfire with 'High Flight'.

John Gillespie Magee Jr, author of 'High Flight'.

John died tragically young, at the controls of a Spitfire, in circumstances that would capture the futility of war and random nature of death in conflict. His passing, however, would succeed in establishing 'High Flight' and thus the legend of the Spitfire. 'High Flight' would go on to be recited by pilots, astronauts and politicians for generations, either in honour of flight or to remember those lost in the endeavour. Such was the gentle power of this pilot's verse that monuments would be erected in his honour and his words carved into stone, cast in metal and taken on paper into space.

'High Flight' was the culmination of an odyssey – a decision to quit a safe and prestigious education in the US and to serve Great Britain, where he'd studied, in the cause against Nazism. America had not yet entered the war when John joined the RCAF and was flying Spitfires, but he would die on the very day his government did declare war – 11 December 1941 – thereby making John officially among the first US casualties of the Second World War.

Born in China in 1922 to missionary parents, an American father John and a British mother Faith, it's arguably this background towards the spiritual that found its way into John's writing and is embodied in 'High Flight'. Attending school initially in China, and learning different languages, John found himself at boarding school in England in the 1930s after his father sent the family abroad for safety as China became embroiled in civil war and conflict with Japan. It was through correspondence with his family while at boarding school that John became a prolific and expressive writer.

Studying at Rugby School in Warwickshire, John further developed his talents, discovering the idealistic Great War poet Rupert Brooke and proceeding to win the Rugby Poetry Prize that Brooke had won in 1905. It was during this time that Magee discovered a kinship with Britain, home to his mother, birthplace of a brother and backdrop to a network of friends and academic encouragement.

It was a fateful decision to travel to the US in the summer of 1939 for an extended break that set John on a two-year path to joining the RCAF and laid the road to 'High Flight'. During that trip, John's passport was inexplicably cancelled, which meant that he could not re-enter Britain. Further, John required a visa to study in Britain but his application was rejected by the US State Department just at a time when the government was concerned about maintaining its neutrality in the face of a looming war while also warning its citizens against travel to potential war zones. Marooned and finishing his education in Connecticut, Magee became convinced his place was in Britain and decided his best option for returning was to join the RAF. With the Battle of Britain raging, in August 1940 John gave up a place at the prestigious Yale University, where he was due to begin in September, and started a campaign to enlist, writing to the Canadian Government and eventually securing an RCAF interview.

John was recommended for training subject to a medical – but there was a hitch. At 6ft (1.8m) the dashing American was tall enough for duty but he was also too skinny and missed the weight requirement by 16lb (7.2kg). Determined not to fall at this first hurdle, Magee stopped smoking and binge-ate to put on the necessary weight. The regimen worked and by January 1941 John found himself on three months' basic training on Fleet Finch and Tiger Moth biplanes at No. 9 Elementary Flying Training School (EFTS) in Ontario – today Niagara District Airport, which contains a stone monument to John. He might have been a literary 18-year-old student with no flying experience, but this period of intense training saw John quickly master the basics and gain the confidence to go solo in half the average time – 6.5 hours.

It was here that John brushed with death. Deliberately entering a vertical spin to test his recovery, he struggled to regain control and his plane corkscrewed 5,000ft (1,500m) in twenty seconds with John pulling out a few hundred feet short of the ground with one final, supreme effort. EFTS was followed by No. 2 Service Flying Training School (SFTS) learning combat and formation flying. Again, John displayed a talent but, again, death was close – thrown clear from a Harvard that he crashed while landing on a night flight. John also got into trouble: lost and landing in a remote spot, he was severely reprimanded for allowing himself to lose the way, failing to calculate the necessary level of fuel and taking too long to return to base. Fears he'd be washed out proved unfounded and John received his wings ten days after his 19th birthday on 19 June 1941. Just over a month later, John's plan was realised and he was back in Britain.

It was in the skies above South Wales where John was sent for training in August 1941 that the young pilot conceived the poem for which he became renowned. Stationed at the RAF's Operational Training Unit (OTU) No. 53 at Llandow in the Vale of Glamorgan, John was assigned a Mk I Spitfire that had served in the Battle of Britain and that, like many of those earlier generations of Spitfires, was being replaced by more advanced models. Flying higher and faster than ever before, John was reluctant to land and his enthusiasm got him grounded for clocking up more hours than his fellow pilots. In a censored letter to a relation, Magee gave a hint of the poem to come. 'I could rhapsodise for pages about the [censored]. It is a thrilling and at the same time terrifying aircraft. It takes off so quickly that before you have recovered from that you are sitting pretty at 5,000 feet,'[7] he wrote. Later, according to John: 'An aeroplane is to us not a weapon of war, but a flash of silver, slanting in the skies; the hum of a deep-voiced motor; a feeling of dizziness; it is speed and ecstasy.'[8]

'High Flight' was written sometime during a training flight in August or September 1941. John claimed to have begun composing it at 30,000ft (9,144m) and to have finished not long after he'd completed the flight, including it in a letter to his parents on thin, blue air-mail paper dated 3 September. 'I have no more news so will stop now. P.T.O for Ditty,'[9] he signed off. That 'ditty' on the other side of the letter was 'High Flight'.

Death finally caught up with this young pilot just a few months later. Stationed with 412 RCAF Squadron at RAF Wellingore, Lincolnshire, John was on a formation training flight with three other Spitfires from his squadron when his Mk VB was struck by a twin-engined Oxford flown by a student pilot. It was a close call for the three other Spitfires, but John had insufficient time to recover. Mid-air collisions were sadly not unusual during the war, even for experienced pilots, and were a sad and futile waste of young life and of much-needed flying and fighting talent. John was laid to rest in the country he'd come to see as home at Scopwick Church, just a few miles from Wellingore.

THE ENGINEERING AND DESIGN THAT MADE THE SPITFIRE SPECIAL

The Spitfire was a cut above the competition and beyond the imagination of any Government official. In its quest to produce the ultimate fighter, Supermarine ignored advice from the Air Ministry, which typically set specifications for aircraft destined for the RAF, and shielded chief designer R.J. Mitchell from official interference. This maverick approach was a success, resulting in a machine that was agile, powerful and responsive. A trinity of elements lay behind this powerful combination: engine, airframe and wing design.

Like other aircraft makers, Supermarine didn't build the engines in its aircraft but partnered with specialist manufacturers – in this case, Rolls-Royce. When designing the Spitfire, R.J. Mitchell picked a Rolls-Royce engine that was still in the development phase, the PV-12. Rolls-Royce would later name the engine models after hunting birds, with Spitfire marques eventually using the Merlin and its successor, the more powerful Griffon. Rolls-Royce engines had driven Mitchell's marine racing aircraft the S.6A and B to high-speed victory in two Schneider Trophy races, in 1929 and 1931, so Mitchell knew their pedigree and potential.

The first Spitfires in May 1938 employed the Merlin I and II, producing up to 1,030hp and capable of a top speed of 362mph (582.5kph) at 18,500ft (5,638m). But Rolls-Royce worked tirelessly to build on these early engines with features and configuration changes that would increase its engines' efficiency, reliability and the amount of power they generated, thereby taking the Spitfire's top speed ever higher and improving performance at different altitudes. The Griffon – introduced to the RAF with the Spitfire Mk XII – was a step change, initially hitting 397mph (638.9kph) at 18,000ft (5,486m) but by the last of the Spitfires it was delivering 2,050hp and speeds of up to 454mph (730kph) at 26,000ft (7,924m).

Rolls-Royce didn't make aircraft engines purely for Supermarine. From the early days of Spitfire development, other manufacturers were aware of the company's work and of the PV-12's potential. Sydney Camm of Hawker Siddeley, building the Hurricane at the same time also in answer to the Air Ministry request, factored the PV-12 into his design. But even though Camm's Hurricane used the Merlin, Mitchell's plane was the faster and offered better performance. The reason? Design.

The PV-12 was a liquid-cooled, inline engine, meaning its cylinders were arranged in two parallel rows, enabling planes to have a narrower profile and thus be more aerodynamic. This broke with a generation of air-cooled engines that had their cylinders set in a circular, or radial, layout and that dominated biplanes and other aircraft of the day. The radial design delivered the distinctive rounded and less aerodynamic front-on profile of the biplane.

But while Camm's Hurricane also featured the PV-12 and also benefited from a narrower profile, the design and manufacturing choices made by Camm limited the potential of the Hurricane, whereas a series of bolder choices by Mitchell facilitated a more streamlined and aerodynamic aircraft. Hawker was a successful maker of biplanes and the Hurricane evolved from that lineage, with a traditional wood and metal construction. Mitchell, however, broke with the biplane entirely by embracing metal and using a monocoque construction method: the Spitfire was made of a skeleton of duraluminium frames to which was attached a duraluminium skin.

The metal skin improved speed and performance, allowing smoother air flow over the aircraft's surfaces. The skin of many aircraft, including the Hurricane, was a type of fabric with a far more irregular surface that would interrupt air flow and therefore produce slightly more drag. The Spitfire's drag factor was further reduced through a form of riveting rarely used in aircraft production to hold metal sheets to the underlying skeleton. Ordinarily, rivet heads would have sat above the surface of the skin, producing a bump, but Mitchell employed flush riveting found at that time on a German pre-war aircraft – the Heinkel He 70 transport. Supermarine's chief aerodynamicist Beverley Shenstone is said to have stumbled upon the Heinkel He 70 at an airshow.

Flush riveting was an expensive and relatively time-consuming process but it delivered vital incremental improvement. Supermarine experiments during development involved gluing split peas over sunken rivets. Completely covered, the aircraft lost 22mph (35.4kph) of speed through drag. Flush riveting was used with compound curves and blended joints to minimise any obtruding edges or surfaces that might inhibit air flow and therefore produce drag. And it paid off: during development, the Spitfire's profile drag – wings, fuselage and tail – was initially calculated at 32.2lb at 100ft/s versus the Hurricane's 40.5lb.

Mitchell's use of monocoque was another example of breaking with the biplane norm. Traditionally, an internal frame of supports and wires maintained an aircraft's shape and bore the stresses and strains of flight and fight. The canvas skin would then be attached to the frame. With monocoque, however, metal skin and metal frames were joined and together provided shape and stress loads, thereby doing away with the internal system of frames and wires. This not only helped reduce weight, it further enhanced the streamlined profile made possible by the PV-12. Monocoque was not new – it had been in use since before the First World War – and the construction technique was also used for the Luftwaffe's Messerschmitt

Bf 109, the Spitfire's chief fighter adversary during the Battle of Britain. But for the RAF, monocoque was a departure that meant agility and durability.

The wing is arguably the Spitfire's most distinctive feature. Mitchell adapted the elliptical wing he'd used in his earlier racing seaplanes, with both the leading and trailing wing edges curved for a number of reasons. Elliptical wings produce an extremely efficient flow of air over and under their surfaces to generate lift. The shape also allowed Supermarine to produce a thin yet strong wing, too. The root – the base of the wing near the fuselage – had a surface area wide enough to deliver strength while allowing Mitchell to reduce the wings' thickness and enhance overall aerodynamics.

The shape of the wing has been eulogised over the decades. Beverley Shenstone, who was the creative force behind the wings, recalls Mitchell being nothing but practical in his choice:

I remember once discussing the wing shape with him and he commented: 'I don't give a b**** whether it's elliptical or not, so long as it covers the guns!' The ellipse was simply the shape which allowed us the thinnest possible wing with sufficient room inside to carry the necessary structure and things we wanted to cram in. And it looked nice.[10]

1

THE ROAD TO DISPERSAL

When bombs struck Southampton and Supermarine's flagship Spitfire factories in 1940 it was the culmination of events that had dragged the world to its second major war in less than thirty years. By the time war was declared on 3 September 1939, few could have doubted Britain's destiny was to be attacked – indeed, the nation had been warned they would be bombed and civil defence plans were already in place. For the people of Southampton and the workers of Supermarine busy supplying the Royal Air Force with Spitfires, it was therefore not a matter of if their workplaces would be attacked but when.

Britain had issued the formal declaration of war when Nazi dictator Adolf Hitler failed to respond to Prime Minister Neville Chamberlain's demand that he withdraw his forces from Poland, who Britain had committed to support. Hitler crossed the Polish border on 1 September, with 1.5 million troops supported by 1,300 aircraft. Since Germany's defeat in the First World War nearly three decades earlier, and in contravention of the ensuing peace settlement with Allied powers at the Treaty of Versailles, Germany under Hitler had mechanised, modernised and expanded her military at an incredible pace and scale. In a series of daring strategic gambits, Hitler had also expanded Germany by reclaiming lands ceded under Versailles or by claiming those belonging to others, all in the name of reunification of the German people, of living space and of national pride, to expunge what was viewed as the 'shame' of Versailles. It was this expansionist creed and military force that Hitler brought to bear on Poland in what was known as Blitzkrieg – lightning war – which saw large numbers of well-trained and equipped troops move rapidly, with integrated air support from bombers and fighters. After a decade of ignoring, explaining and attempting to accommodate Hitler to avoid another costly conflict, war had become unavoidable for those who valued liberty and freedom.

Hitler seemed unstoppable. Such was the devastating combination of speed and force – combined with the active collusion of the forces of the Soviet Union – that Poland could do little but surrender after twenty-six days. A brief period of relative calm that followed was shattered in spring 1940 when Hitler again unleashed Blitzkrieg, this time on the countries of northern and western Europe, conquering in a rapid series of actions Norway, Luxembourg, the Netherlands, Belgium and – finally – in June 1940, the great imperial power France, British ally and long-time German foe. Half of Europe lay defeated, with cities burning and millions dead or displaced, and Britain alone among the nations of Europe who were neither neutral, Fascist nor occupied. The inescapable conclusion was that Britain was next, a feeling intensified by the bitter taste left by Dunkirk that marked the sorry end to Britain's forces' first engagement with Hitler's military. Ten divisions had been dispatched to Belgium and France as the British Expeditionary Force (BEF) in an attempt to thwart the German advance. If the BEF's commanders had expected to be able to reproduce the blocking action of the Great War, they were to be bitterly disappointed. Heavily outnumbered and let down by poor leadership and terrible communications, defeats and reversals culminated in the evacuation of 338,000 British and French troops from the Belgian seaside town of Dunkirk in a makeshift fleet of 800 naval and civilian craft.

With German forces now poised just across the Channel, attack and invasion of the British mainland according to the blueprint of Blitzkrieg seemed close at hand. The prevailing military wisdom of that era had it that an enemy would try to undermine the morale and fighting spirit of populations through massive aerial bombing of urban centres and, as time wore on, experience seemed to bear out such thinking as German bombers smashed Poland's capital, Warsaw. Before that, the German Air Force had supported the Fascist General Franco during the Spanish Civil War. In one infamous incident, in April 1937, aircraft of the German Condor Legion had bombed the sleepy market town of Guernica for three straight hours in an attack that would claim the lives of an estimated 1,650 civilians and become a poster-child for infamy.

Viewing this seemingly unstoppable catastrophe on the Continent, the British Government enacted a series of measures designed to protect the cities and the citizenry. On the day German forces crossed the border into Poland, the British Government activated its plan to evacuate children from British cities. More than 1.5 million children started the trek by train to the safety of homes in villages, towns and rural locations. Steps were also taken to protect British cities against the kinds of bomber raids that had devastated Poland with the introduction of a blackout on 1 September. Homes, shops, businesses and factories were all required during night-time hours to black up their windows and not allow even a chink of light to leak out and act as a potential beacon to the enemy overhead. The blackout was enforced by civilian Air Raid Precautions (ARP) wardens, a force formed before the war as events had turned ever darker on the continental mainland. Every night its members paced the streets of Britain to enforce the blackout.

The expected bombings did not materialise – at least not initially – and with the nation slowly catching its breath, nearly half the evacuated children had returned home by January 1940. But if there were any doubts as to Hitler's intentions, they would be shattered by Germany's dizzying assault on the West and its rapid series of successes during spring 1940. With mainland Europe under his heel, Hitler inevitably turned his attention to Britain. Issuing Führer Directive No. 16 on 16 July, he instructed his commanders to execute Operation Sea Lion, the invasion of Britain that was to begin – they were ordered – by no later than 15 September that year. Hitler made one final offer of peace in a radio broadcast of 19 July but, unsurprisingly, this was roundly rejected. The countdown for the war coming to Britain was officially running and there was nowhere left to hide.

Operation Sea Lion was to run in two stages: the first was for Hitler's Luftwaffe to eliminate the Royal Air Force and achieve control of the skies above Great Britain. Next would begin the invasion: ground landings, with millions of German troops crossing the English Channel on barges protected from above by the Luftwaffe, who would deliver close support once the fighting started. Hitler was unequivocal in his expectations with regards to the RAF. In Directive No. 16 he stated: 'The English Air Force must be so reduced morally and physically that it is unable to

Hitler's Luftwaffe pounded key targets in Southampton.

deliver any significant attack against the German crossing.' The date he set for this was mid-August and, on paper, the RAF's fate must have seemed inescapable. The RAF was smaller than the Luftwaffe overall and it possessed fewer fighters: 1,468 RAF aircraft in total at the start of July 1940, of which 754 were single-seaters such as the Spitfire, compared with 3,841 and 1,107 respectively for the German Air Force.[11] The Luftwaffe's pilots also had greater combat experience compared with RAF crews: a number of German pilots had fought in air-to-air and air-to-ground settings and practised formation flying during the Spanish Civil War, and they had been an integral part of Blitzkrieg across Western Europe.

Fate moved a step closer to Southampton and the workers and factories producing Spitfires on 13 August, Adlertag (Eagle Day), the beginning of what would become known as the Battle of Britain that saw the Luftwaffe's armada unleashed. Battle commenced with a ten-hour assault that probed the defences and struck targets across southern England. In the crosshairs were RAF bases, runways and airfields, radar stations and – of course – the aircraft and pilots. Southampton suffered its first damage, but got off extremely lightly compared with what was in store. But the aerial battle didn't go entirely as planned for the Germans. The fighting capabilities of the RAF were bolstered by growing numbers of Spitfires. Among its crews were large numbers of very experienced and highly determined Polish and Czech pilots who'd escaped occupied Europe and who would count for more than 20 per cent of RAF aircrews during the Battle of Britain. The RAF's chances were further enhanced through the use of technology: the relatively new Chain Home radar system was an early warning system capable of spotting incoming formations, meaning Fighter Command could have planes in the air and ready to intercept. The Luftwaffe's radio signals were intercepted, too, by the legendary code breakers at Bletchley Park.

The Germans made mistakes, too. The Messerschmitt Bf 109 from brilliant German aircraft designer Willy Messerschmitt was then the Luftwaffe's best and most lethal combat plane. The interceptor-fighter had been in development since the 1930s and was a veteran of the Spanish Civil War, allowing Messerschmitt time to fine tune his machine. It posed a serious challenge to the Spitfire but it was handicapped by the Luftwaffe command's decision during the Battle of Britain that it should support slower-moving bombers whose mission was to hit strategic targets such as airfields and Fighter Command centres, and which were vulnerable to attack from faster-moving aircraft such as the Spitfire. This curtailed the freedom of the Messerschmitts to engage one-on-one against the Spitfire.

The Luftwaffe also massively overestimated its own success in terms of numbers of RAF aircraft lost and the amount of damage its bombers had inflicted on Fighter Command's infrastructure. It was a calculation that would have profound consequences, as the Luftwaffe shifted its tactics at a pivotal point during the Battle of Britain in the mistaken belief it had achieved its goal of decimating the RAF. The darkest day for RAF Fighter Command came on 31 August, with thirty-nine aircraft shot down and fourteen pilots killed – the single worst casualty rate for the whole of the Battle of Britain. The Fighter Command building and airfield at Biggin Hill, guarding the approach to London from the South-East, sustained such cumulative damage that they were put out of action, with command of the aircraft based there assigned to other Fighter Command centres.

Calculating incorrectly that the RAF was on its last legs, Luftwaffe commander Herman Göring switched from targeting airfields to bombing London on 7 September, striking the docks and industrial centres of the East End in a sustained raid of nearly twelve hours. The raid, which became known as Black Saturday, involved hundreds of bombers and fighter escorts and left 448 dead. Göring's shift to urban attacks relieved the crews, airfields and installations of the RAF, giving them time to rebuild cratered runways and shattered buildings and to regroup as a fighting force, but it also meant that the days were numbered for Southampton and its Spitfire factories. London had been bombed before during the Second World War but Black Saturday signalled the large-scale and co-ordinated bombing of major British cities known as the Blitz. Two weeks after London, German bombs found their way to the Spitfire factories.

Southampton had a long and illustrious history as a centre of industry and shipping. Founded on the wide banks of the River Itchen, which empties into the Solent, Southampton had grown and prospered in serving military and commercial shipping over the centuries. The birth of aviation at the dawn of the twentieth century opened a fresh chapter in the city's history, as a new generation of adventurers and entrepreneurs rushed to make money in aircraft manufacturing. So it was that aircraft construction came to the city in 1913 when one of those early pioneers, Noel Pemberton-Billing, founded the eponymous Pemberton-Billing to build floatplanes – aircraft that could take off or land on water and which served both civilian and military markets.

Three years after it started, Pemberton-Billing was renamed Supermarine, having been bought by works manager Hubert Scott-Paine, who had the vision to hire a promising and talented young designer named Reginald Joseph – better known as R.J. – Mitchell. It was Mitchell who made his name working on a series of racing planes for Supermarine that competed in and won the internationally acclaimed Schneider Trophy race. In 1928 the company changed hands when it was bought by the aviation division of Vickers-Armstrongs, a huge and acquisitive corporation that spanned armaments, shipbuilding and military vehicles. Overnight, the little builder of wood and fabric floatplanes had become a serious cog in the British military's supply network. Not long after acquisition, Mitchell would start work developing a fighter aircraft that would confront the Luftwaffe in the skies above Britain less than a decade later.

Mitchell started work on the Spitfire in answer to a call from the Aircraft Ministry – which was responsible for the RAF's contracts, procurement and administrative affairs – for a mono-wing interceptor-fighter. He eventually put forward a design based on those Schneider Trophy-winning sea racers so compelling that the Ministry rewrote its original technical requirements to fit Mitchell's plane, landing Supermarine a £2 million order in 1936 for 310 of the Spitfire Mk I type for delivery fifteen months later. It was to be the biggest single order in the company's history and would elevate significantly its importance in the British military supply system, bringing the former floatplane maker to the attention of the politicians, military commanders, civil servants, the media and the public.

It was an order Supermarine would also struggle to fulfil, so management took steps to expand. The existing red-brick Woolston works saw the addition of a magnificent, gleaming white art deco extension that incorporated a new design workshop and a stunning hangar, complete with a slipway into the river for seaplanes. In 1938 ground was broken on the new Itchen works, a few hundred yards away, and completed the following year. Built on land purchased from the Southern Gas Company and Ship Builders, Itchen was sandwiched between the river and a railway line.

Supermarine had expanded physically but deliveries of those first Spitfires was late. A specialist in wood-framed floatplanes, Supermarine was short of the skilled metal workers and riveters it needed for mass production of this all-metal plane. Further, staff were at capacity fulfilling an expansion in orders for flying boats and amphibious aircraft. Supermarine contracted out sub-assemblies such as wings and tail sections to outside firms, with subcontractors also providing smaller parts. The Spitfire was an ambitious new design employing new materials and new manufacturing techniques, so suppliers struggled, with the wing sub-assemblies causing most issues with production. Supermarine therefore missed its initial delivery deadline and the first Mk 1 didn't roll out until August 1938. With the threat from Nazi Germany growing, the RAF was becoming frantic at the delays and the Government was taking flak for leaving the Air Force unprepared.

Radical action was deemed necessary and Southampton nearly lost its status as the jewel in the crown of Spitfire production as the Air Ministry turned to Britain's car industry for help. Car makers, it was felt, possessed the necessary expertise and management experience of modern mass production to successfully make weapons and deliver the Spitfire quickly and at volume.

The Government engaged industrialist and philanthropist William Morris, 1st Viscount of Nuffield and founder of car giant Morris Motors. Morris boasted he could design and construct a brand new factory capable of producing sixty Spitfires a week – four times greater than anybody else. With Supermarine behind on orders, in April 1938 the Ministry awarded Morris a £7 million contract to deliver 1,000 Spitfires – another record-breaking order for one type of aircraft produced in Britain.

But Morris would not deliver and it soon became clear that car manufacturers were demonstrably not ready to handle the unique demands of the Spitfire. A year after Morris landed his record-breaking contract he'd failed to deliver a single plane, with the company's delayed Castle Bromwich factory not producing its first Spitfire until the eve of the Battle of Britain in June 1940. Output would eventually count handsomely towards the war effort, with Castle Bromwich producing 13,000 Spitfires, but by the time of the Battle of Britain it was hitting nowhere near the levels expected by a desperate RAF and frantic Government. This left the burden for supply of the majority of Spitfires squarely on the shoulders of two highly exposed, easily identifiable and critically important factories in Southampton. A devastating blow against one or both of these would therefore have profound and possibly fatal consequences for the RAF and the nation.

Supermarine undertook massive expansion of its existing Woolston factory to handle record-breaking Government orders for Spitfires.

Supermarine's Southampton factories were the centre of the nation's Spitfire production but the Luftwaffe raids of 26 September signalled the death knell for Woolston and Itchen (here, before and after).

For the Luftwaffe pilots who'd switched from duelling with the 'vanquished' RAF to attempting to pound the population of Britain into submission and break its industrial will through intensive bombing, Southampton was a clear target. Moreover, the Supermarine factories represented easy pickings: not only was Woolston easy to identify from the air thanks to that white art deco extension but it also lay in very close proximity to the Itchen plant. Nearby, too, was the mighty Thornycroft shipbuilders turning out corvettes and destroyers for the Royal Navy. Add to that a gas works, electric power station and a nearby railway station and you had a tidy package of high-value military manufacturing targets and utilities located in a densely packed civilian area. Casualties and damage to infrastructure would be considerable.

Southampton had been bombed earlier but September saw the beginning of a chain of events that would lead to Supermarine breaking up its Spitfire manufacturing and embarking on a radical and unique experiment in wartime industrial production. In August the Luftwaffe had started to target the factories of aircraft manufacturers turning out the fighters and bombers vital to the defence of Britain. On 11 September, a small force of German bombers dropped their payload a few miles outside the city centre on Eastleigh airfield, where Supermarine staff assembled Spitfire subcomponents in preparation for dispatch to RAF combat units and bases. The Luftwaffe's bombs narrowly missed the Supermarine flight shed and assembly hangars with their newly finished Spitfires ready for delivery, but they did succeed in striking the nearby Cunliffe-Owen factory used to repair Spitfires – killing fifty-two workers and injuring ninety-two.

Four days later, on 15 September, the Luftwaffe were back with a force of thirty aircraft, half bombers, to take out those Supermarine factories. Between them they released 12 tonnes of bombs over the Supermarine works and also Thornycroft but, miraculously, damage to the Supermarine buildings was superficial. Disruption to Spitfire production was equally minimal, too, with just a single night shift lost. But the civilians living close by in the streets surrounding the works bore the brunt: six people were killed, 125 homes destroyed and more than 1,000 damaged. Warning bells began to sound for Supermarine's management over the apparent vulnerability of its prized factories. A plan was needed for the sake of continued Spitfire production.

The Luftwaffe returned on 24 September This time a force of thirty-seven bombers, with fighter escort, struck Woolston and Itchen, the gas works and electricity power plants and the central railway station. There had been little warning and Supermarine workers labouring at their benches rushed to the supposed safety of a long row of specially built surface shelters sited in a meadow on Peartree Green, which lay to the east of a railway line that separated them from the plants on Hazel Road. Access to Peartree Green was via a narrow passage that cut through the railway embankment. The late warning and the long distance to Peartree Green would have tragic consequences as many didn't make the shelter and took refuge in the cut-through tunnel, where they lost their lives following a direct hit that reduced the bridge to a pile of rubble. A large number who did make it to the shelter lost their lives, too, after it sustained a direct hit. Many more couldn't even get out of the factories: knots of people pressed into the factories' narrow exits, which quickly became overwhelmed in the rush. That left workers diving beneath heavy workbenches to seek shelter as the bombs started to fall. Those who decided to make a dash for it during a pause in bombing emerged to find a scene of devastation and horror.

But the Luftwaffe was not done with the home of the Spitfire and on 26 September German bombers unleashed a decisive blow that would end the part played by Woolston and Itchen in Supermarine's manufacturing story. Sixty bombers with escorts struck the gas works, docks and Supermarine factories, with workers once more struggling to make good their escape, trying to squeeze through doorways that were again backed up. This time the air raid shelters were given a wide berth and people found what cover they could so that, when the shelters did suffer another hit, there was no repeat of the 24 September catastrophe.

The raids resulted in seventeen workers killed but the Luftwaffe had, miraculously, failed to land the decisive blow its commanders had expected. Much of the special equipment – jigs and tools – and the valuable material used to assemble Spitfires was salvageable. Supermarine's design office, which housed vital technical drawings of current and future planned designs, had had a remarkable escape. At least two bombs had struck the suite, with one passing through the window and hitting the mud on the riverbank outside, while another passed through the floor without exploding. It was a close shave for the designs and blueprints, without which current and future manufacturing of new Spitfire types could not have proceeded so smoothly. The walls and metal roof beams of the factories had also survived the blasts and flames, but these facts could not save Woolston and Itchen and within twenty-four hours of the Luftwaffe's raid another force struck that would end production of Spitfires in Southampton and see Supermarine take its manufacturing underground. The Government's new Minister of Aircraft Production, Lord Beaverbrook, descended on Southampton and decided to safeguard future supplies of Spitfires by ordering the dispersal of production across a network of hidden and secret factories.

Beaverbrook was a new minister leading a new government department, the Ministry of Aircraft Production. It had been created by Churchill to solve problems of supplying the RAF that had emerged during the Battle of Britain. Beaverbrook,

Small businesses such as the Wessex Garage in Salisbury were carefully selected as bases for secret Spitfire production.

appointed by Churchill to head up this important new ministry, was a controversial choice. A Cabinet minister during the Great War, he had experience of government but, as a press baron who owned the *Sunday* and *Daily Express* newspapers, he came with a colourful reputation for making and breaking people. Churchill, however, had known Beaverbrook for decades and appeared to recognise in him an individual capable of bringing energy and determination to the role. A Civil Service outsider, Beaverbrook would break rules and use his very personal and rather direct style to achieve results in the dusty corridors and dingy meeting rooms of officialdom. And so it was Beaverbrook who departed from the convention of repairing and resuming production by ordering the dispersal of Supermarine's Spitfire manufacturing – breaking up the construction of wings, fuselages and other sections and assemblies across a network of small sites.

But while Beaverbrook is synonymous with the factory dispersal, it wasn't entirely his idea: a blueprint had already been developed by Supermarine's rather less well-known works manager, Hartley Blyth Pratt, in recognition of the growing menace posed to production by bombing. Pratt's plan had also been partly activated. Before the fatal raids, a German reconnaissance mission over Southampton and the dropping of the first bombs on the city on 20 June had highlighted the risk to Supermarine factories. A burst of anti-aircraft fire resulted in a chunk of shell striking the facilities at Woolston, narrowly missing a worker. The factories were clearly vulnerable and that left Supermarine's warning antenna twitching.

Pratt's plan was simple, albeit small-scale compared with what Beaverbrook authorised. He envisaged a network of small, covert factories across Southampton, operating inside a range of everyday premises that would mean they were suitably camouflaged to outsiders, thus allowing Spitfire manufacturing to continue unobserved and unmolested. Should a bomber succeed in striking one of these smaller units then the hope was that any damage to overall Spitfire production would be relatively contained. The search was on for city sites that would be hard for the enemy to identify but that had sufficient capacity for industrial production. The first picked were Hendy's Garage off Pound Tree Road and Seward Garage on the Winchester Road in Shirley. Storage was found at the Weston Rolling Mills in Southampton, the brickworks at Bishops Waltham and on the Leigh Road in Eastleigh. Accounts moved to Deepdene in Bitterne Park, and ministry inspection was relocated to Holt House in Chandlers Ford. But jigs, which were vital to the construction of Spitfires, did not move straight away for fear of disrupting production.

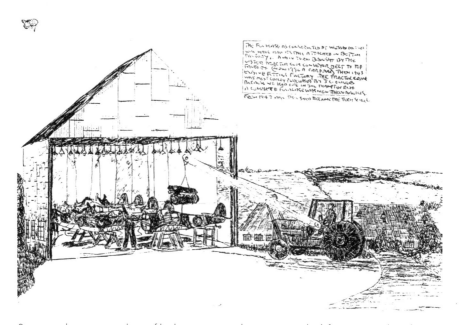

Some production moved out of built-up areas and into purpose-built factories, such as this one sketched by milk boy Ken Hayter, at Old Sarum.

The raid of 15 September altered that. The equipment vital to building Spitfires began its migration, while it was also decided to identify more sites around Southampton capable of housing these covert factories. Supermarine's general manager, Wilf Elliott, authorised the requisitioning of a second wave of buildings – Lowther's Garage in Shirley, the Sunlight Laundry and Hants & Dorset Bus Depot, both on Winchester Road in Shirley, and the Hollybrook Stores nearby on Hollybrook Road. Southampton would grow to become the single largest dispersal network – comprising twenty-seven secret factories. The 26 September raid changed things again. Whether Woolston and Itchen could have been salvaged was debatable; structurally, they remained intact while paper designs, equipment, supplies and assembled components all survived the bombing. But Beaverbrook seemed unwilling to gamble and so ordered Supermarine to abandon Woolston and Itchen with dispersal to facilities that would be requisitioned by his powerful department.

Supermarine's management swung into action. From the fourth floor of the nearby Polygon Hotel, near the docks, Vickers Supermarine's production team under works manager Len Gooch began to put into practice a larger-scale version of Pratt's earlier plan. Pratt was no longer in position, having been left not just physically wounded but psychologically damaged by the carnage he'd witnessed during the raid of 24 September. Such was the trauma experienced by Pratt he would later take his own life.

The strategy radically expanded Pratt's Southampton concept, to take in a 50-mile (80km) radius of the city. The objective was to identify sites within that area that offered the potential for self-contained Spitfire production, with plants expected to carry out some facet of the production line process – from sub- to final assembly, testing and delivery. Armed with a set of Ordnance Survey maps and accompanied by a uniformed policeman to enforce the law if necessary, Supermarine engineers were dispatched in a car to scout locations capable of meeting the criteria. Buildings were deemed suitable based on size and space and whether their construction and available power supply could support the equipment needed to build fuselages or wings. Sites needed to have concrete floors, good-sized doors and be roomy and uncluttered by pillars. Car dealerships, bus depots and garages were ideal candidates, with the latter in particular suitable thanks to their high roofs that could accommodate the large jigs for wing construction. Other popular options were warehouses, rolling mills, laundries and a factory for making – yes – strawberry baskets.

Three areas were finally selected outside Southampton: Salisbury, Reading and Trowbridge. Salisbury would become the most productive. Each was fed by a network of factories in surrounding towns and cities – up to sixty-five units in total –

that would replicate the functions of the different shops and manufacturing stages of production at Woolston and Itchen and the hangars at Eastleigh Airport. Factories in the network had clearly defined roles and functions working towards the final goal of delivering finished aircraft. They were to build Spitfire sub-assemblies such as fuselages, wing leading edges or complete wings, and tail units, that would eventually be transported by truck to facilities at one of a series of special airfields for final assembly and test flight ahead of delivery to waiting RAF commands around the country.

Dispersal brought communication challenges. Supermarine had been a close-knit organisation in Southampton with almost every branch located within just a few hundred yards of each other, enabling design, planning and production to interact on a daily basis. Supply challenges during the 1930s had arisen when parts of the Spitfire's production had been outsourced to subcontractors. Dispersal threatened a recurrence of these problems as design, works management and production would be in different locations. It was therefore decided to establish a new headquarters for works, administration and design. The place chosen was Hursley House, a 350-acre estate and eighteenth-century mansion on the edge of the Hampshire Downs between Winchester, Southampton and Romsey. Hursley was supported by offices at Winchester and Chandler's Ford.

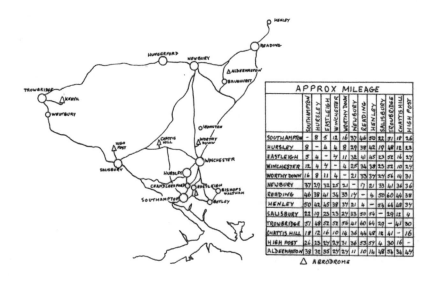

APPROX MILEAGE	SOUTHAMPTON	HURSLEY	EASTLEIGH	WINCHESTER	WORTHY DOWN	NEWBURY	READING	HENLEY	SALISBURY	TROWBRIDGE	CHATTIS HILL	HIGH POST
SOUTHAMPTON	-	8	5	12	16	37	46	50	22	51	18	26
HURSLEY	8	-	4	4	8	29	38	42	19	48	12	23
EASTLEIGH	5	4	-	4	11	32	41	45	23	52	16	27
WINCHESTER	12	4	4	-	4	25	34	38	23	52	10	27
WORTHY DOWN	16	8	11	4	-	21	33	37	27	56	14	31
NEWBURY	37	29	32	25	21	-	17	21	33	41	34	36
READING	46	38	41	34	33	17	-	4	50	60	44	38
HENLEY	50	42	45	38	37	21	4	-	54	64	48	37
SALISBURY	22	19	23	23	27	33	50	54	-	29	12	4
TROWBRIDGE	57	48	52	52	56	41	60	64	29	-	41	30
CHATTIS HILL	18	12	16	10	14	36	44	48	12	41	-	16
HIGH POST	26	23	27	27	31	36	53	57	4	30	16	-
ALDERMASTON	38	32	35	24	24	11	10	14	48	54	34	47

△ AERODROME

A network of more than sixty facilities, spanning assembly, parts and airfields ran from Southampton via Salisbury to Trowbridge and Reading and encompassing the towns and villages in-between – captured in this hand-drawn map.

Identifying suitable locations was one thing, but obtaining them was another and officials encountered a variety of responses. Supermarine was attempting to take over the premises of functioning businesses – something owners could quite understandably resist. Others who were aware of the fates of Woolston and Itchen were uneasy about the prospect of having a Spitfire factory on their doorsteps, lest it make them a target for enemy bombing. In other cases, Supermarine ran into departmental politics where local officials raised objections, or where rival government departments had beaten Beaverbrook's department to the punch on requisition.

Supermarine was backed by the power of a requisition order from Beaverbrook's Ministry of Aircraft Production whose considerations, the minister had firmly established, trumped those of all other departments. Requisition negated the need to negotiate with owners and helped Supermarine's managers slice through the legal complexities and delays of needing to obtain a lease. Requisitions, however, weren't always met with equanimity or acceptance and sometimes business owners held out. On at least two occasions a secret Spitfire factory would share premises with its peacetime operators, with the result that a wall had to be built across the factory floors to separate the two concerns. Other times where rival officials or departments had beaten Supermarine to prime locations, negotiations with rivals were called for. The Hants & Dorset Bus Garage in Shirley was a particularly coveted site because of its high ceilings that in peacetime had helped accommodate buses and that, for the purposes of Spitfire construction, afforded vital space for the wing jigs. The Ministry of Supply and Air Raid Precautions had bagged the site as a store for sandbags but Supermarine needed the garage's space to help make the rather more useful Spitfire wings.

Hursley House proved a more genteel, if ultimately sadder, affair in this era of requisitions. In 1940 the estate owner, widowed Lady Mary Cooper, was preparing to reprise her home's role during the Great War as a convalescent home for wounded officers. The death in May 1940 of her husband, Sir George Alexander Cooper, meant both home and grounds were the sole domains of Lady Cooper and her servants. The Ministry of Aircraft Production, however, saw Hursley House and grounds, which were hidden from the Luftwaffe on the edge of the peaceful Hampshire Downs, as playing a much more vital and integral part in the war effort. After a temporary stint at Southampton University, the Supermarine design team, whose work had so narrowly escaped incineration on the night of 24 September, was relocated to Hursley after the building and a portion of the grounds were requisitioned by the Ministry.

Lady Cooper welcomed Supermarine staff in style on 7 December 1940, with a floral bouquet in the shape of a Spitfire, but her home soon changed radically.

Among the initial changes, rooms became offices and the stables a lab for prototype testing. In came draughtsmen, tracers, mathematicians and aerodynamicists – all under the watchful eye of Supermarine's chief designer Joe Smith. Panelling and plaques were boarded up and works of art removed to storage.

As the design team expanded, a hangar was erected to house the design draughtsmen of the drawing office, while the mathematicians and aerodynamicists of the technical office took over more of the house. Hursley was a hub of Spitfire innovation, design and testing. It was no surprise then that the facilities should be expanded and a second hangar was duly erected in the stately grounds to house a brand-new experimental department, for construction of prototypes of new each new version of the Spitfire on-site, ahead of testing. As the top-secret design and experimental work expanded, so the domestic arrangements became impractical and Lady Cooper's house-sharing days numbered. Just two years after her floral welcome and following a fire that succeeded in highlighting the security risks posed to Supermarine at Hursley, Lady Cooper was asked – nicely – to leave late in 1942. She obliged and never returned.

Sourcing buildings suitable for aircraft construction was just one half of Supermarine's challenge. Southampton aside, dispersal had seen secret factories deliberately placed in buildings that occupied relatively quiet locations away from major population centres to avoid both the Luftwaffe and the public's attention. But while it had the buildings, Supermarine lacked the workers to fill them. Even before the Luftwaffe struck, Supermarine was experiencing a shortage of employees skilled in the new techniques needed to build Mitchell's revolutionary fighter. The September raids made things worse.

And while Supermarine had begun shifting vital plant and equipment to the secret sites outside Southampton, not all the remaining workers from those original factories were willing or able to follow. Those not personally dealing with mental or physical injuries, or loss of homes, were helping less fortunate family members. There was a reluctance, too, to leave families in Southampton as it felt like they'd be abandoning them to more bombing. Their fears would prove prescient as Southampton had been earmarked for attention by the Luftwaffe. German bombers struck repeatedly in the months following, peaking at the end of November 1940 with raids of up to seven hours in length and involving 120 bombers. Such was the pyre ignited it was possible to see the glow of the flames in the sky from across the Channel in Cherbourg on the French coast.

Another factor holding people back from following Supermarine was the lack of suitable housing in the dispersal areas. The need to provide accommodation had become almost as high a priority as finding and setting up the secret factories themselves. All told, by December 1940, the employee headcount had fallen to

3,079 from 3,660 in September. The designers, draughtsmen and tracers tried to find lodgings for them and their families in Hursley or nearby villages. Conditions were cramped, with stories of families occupying just one room in small cottages. Bus transport was provided for design team staff so that they could commute between Hursley and Southampton, but many sought accommodation locally to find respite from the bombing of Southampton. At one airfield assembly and test site, High Post, the flying club's hotel was taken over as accommodation with six railway carriages brought in especially and parked up nearby, with each compartment serving as a bedroom for on-site engineers. With lodgings in critically short supply, Supermarine's parent company, Vickers-Armstrongs, began assembling prefabricated huts for workers and families at Hiltingbury, in the Eastleigh area.

The Luftwaffe's September bombing campaign failed in its command's objective of killing the Spitfire stone dead in its cradle, but it had succeeded in putting a worrying-sized dent in the output of new planes. By the end of 1940, twenty-two workshops were in use and three aerodromes had become available for final assembly and flight testing. Yet, by early 1941, Spitfire production was down by as much as 30 per cent compared with just before the raid, according to Beaverbrook.[12] The effect on output of the bombing of Woolston and Itchen had been exacerbated by the practical and logistical necessities of implementing Beaverbrook's survival plan: equipment and tools vital for construction had to be taken off the production line, shipped out of Southampton and installed at the secret sites scattered across southern England, putting them temporarily out of commission. Along with the equipment went factory hands, seconded to sourcing locations and then fitting out new sites in preparation for production, rather than spending valuable time building Spitfires.

Further, there was the challenge of finding workers to fill these new factories and of getting manufacturing output back up to speed. Dispersal was a brilliant idea. But by their very nature, places such as Salisbury also lacked the huge and ready supply of workers that manufacturers and the military might expect to find in big cities or urban areas such as Southampton. Spitfire production might have been given the kiss of life thanks to the decisive intervention of Beaverbrook, but unless Supermarine found a way to address the labour shortage things would be no further forward and the Luftwaffe would have achieved its goal. Supermarine needed a bold approach and it needed one fast – for the sake of the nation.

SPITFIRE SUPPLY LINES UNCOVERED

BY NORMAN PARKER

Parts and sub-assemblies for Spitfires came from a network of suppliers and subcontractors in addition to Vickers-Armstrongs and Supermarine. Some of the identities of the companies that composed that network are still only now coming to light. The process of researching *Secret Spitfires* took me to the Isle of Wight to examine some of the company's old technical drawings at specialist restoration and repair company, Airframe Assemblies. Hidden among those documents was a list of some of those companies, recorded opposite.

Secret factories contributed to a fleet of more than 20,000 Spitfires, with plants served by a network of hidden parts suppliers.

Company Name	Function
Aero Engines	Tail elevators and tabs, ailerons, chassis pins, tail wheels
Airscrew	Propeller
G. Beaton & Sons	Ribs
Bratt Colbran	Radiator fairings
British Pressed Panels	Fuselage skin plates
British Pressed Steel	Fuselage and wing skin plates
Car Bodies	Engine cowlings, Front cowling ring
Dunlop	Wheels and tyres
Excelsior Motor Radiators	Oil tank, top fuel tank and sumps, cockpit door, chassis fairings, reflector gun-sight mountings, windscreen, pilot's aft windows
Folland Aircraft	Pilot's seat, frame 19, rear fuselage
General Aircraft	Engine hand controls, wing tips, cartridge boxes
Heston Aircraft	Wing flaps
J. Samuel White	Radiator flaps, locking levers for flap cylinders, frames 8 and 11
Oddie B&C	Pilot's controls, aerial details
Pobjoy Motors	Gun mountings, rudder and trim flap
Pye Radio	Flap and elevator trim controls
Reston	Main fuselage frames
Serck Radiators	Header tank
Singers Motors	Engine mountings, aileron control drums, rudder-control pulleys, aileron connection rods and link assemblies
Supermarine	Main fuselage and nose section
Vickers-Armstrongs	Oleos
Westland Aircraft	Ribs
Williamson	Lower fuel tank
Worcester Sheet Metal	Gun tunnels
Wyndham Hewitt	Rudder bias assembly

RACE AND REACTION: BIRTH OF THE SPITFIRE

BY NORMAN PARKER

The Spitfire can trace its ancestry back to the early 1930s when Supermarine's mono-wing floatplanes won the prestigious Schneider Trophy for Britain and, in so doing, established the world air speed record. The Schneider Trophy was a race for seaplanes conceived by industrialist and aviation enthusiast Jacques Schneider and first run in 1913. Winning the Trophy was a source of great national pride for governments and bred intense competition among manufacturers, who'd push their designs to the limit.

Supermarine had crashed out on its first attempt to win the Trophy in 1925 with an S.4 running a Napier engine and designed by Supermarine's Reginald Joseph (R.J.) Mitchell. Not to be defeated, Mitchell went on to design the S.5 and the Rolls-Royce-powered S.6A and S.6B, which together would win three Schneider races in a row and secure Britain the Trophy in perpetuity. The outcome of the races underlined the woeful inadequacy of the Royal Air Force's fleet, with an S.6B breaking records and, in a later more powerful incarnation, going on to become the first aircraft ever to break the 400mph (643kph) barrier.

The Air Ministry, responsible for the administrative affairs of the RAF, would issue a specification – F7/30 – for a next-generation fighter. Among the highlights of this specification: a single-seater day and night fighter capable of having the highest possible rate of climb; the highest possible speed at 15,000ft (4,572m); fighting view; capability of easy and rapid production in quantity; and ease of maintenance. It was to be powered by an officially approved engine.

A handful of companies successfully responded to the specification but just three moved beyond the initial submission to testing: the Westland Aircraft with its PV4, which would eventually fail to hit the RAF's performance requirements so would not continue into production; the Gloster Aircraft Company's SS37 that became the successful Gloster Gladiator; and Supermarine with the Type 224 from Mitchell. Supermarine's plane was one of only two in the F7/30 line-up whose designer had departed from the standard biplane design common to that era, with the Type 224 employing a cranked – or inverted – gull wing. It was, however, the only mono-wing plane in that F7/30 parade to actually make it through to testing. Featuring a fixed undercarriage and an open cockpit in addition to the gull wing, the Type 224 echoed Mitchell's earlier sea racers and looked nothing like the Spitfire we know. After many changes to the original design, the aeroplane was built, making

The rise of Adolf Hitler, here with Luftwaffe chief Herman Göring, helped set the RAF on course for the Spitfire.

its maiden flight on 20 February 1934. Subsequent testing proved to be most disappointing. Despite fitting an improved Goshawk engine and extending the wings to overcome high wing-loading and providing room for the steam cooling system, the design was not a success. The engine was unreliable, being at risk of overheating, and slower than the S.6B – factors that contributed to all work being cancelled on 9 January 1935. The Type 224 was finally moved to the military base at Orford Ness, Suffolk, and used as a gunnery target.

It was a setback for Supermarine, but not the end of testing and development, which had continued as a private venture, without Ministry backing. Mitchell had decided it would be better to improve the original specification around a promising new engine, the PV-12 from Rolls-Royce, which would become the Merlin. The company decided to depart from the Ministry's official brief and build a killer fighter rather than allow itself to be restricted by a set of specifications cooked up by a committee at the Air Ministry. Supermarine worked in collaboration with Rolls-Royce on the endeavour, and the result was the Type 300 that Supermarine submitted to the Air Ministry for consideration in July 1934. The Air Ministry accepted the revised scheme and in December 1934 issued a new specification around Mitchell's design: specification number F37/34.

With the rise of Nazism in Germany and that country's rearmament, the timing was portentous. Just the year before, Adolf Hitler had been appointed Chancellor of Germany and withdrawn his country from the League of Nations. Setting about rearmament, he created a German Air Ministry and it swiftly commissioned a prototype from a German aircraft manufacturer that years later would become the Messerschmitt Bf 109 and go head-to-head against the Spitfire in the Battle of Britain. That battle would be overseen by Hitler's air chief, Luftwaffe commander Herman Göring.

Having been officially accepted, a single prototype Type 300 was built to an official Air Ministry contract and given the service serial number K5054. A wooden mock-up was constructed to develop the layout and would hang from the roof in Supermarine's experimental department workshop in Southampton long after the real thing overtook it. The prototype was entirely hand-built. The construction frame – called a jig – used for the fuselage carried the internal shaping frames that, along with the wing ribs, would have been built individually as bench-built sub-assemblies. The final skin installations were hand-rolled individually by highly skilled sheet metal workers to suit the variable contours of the emerging fighter aircraft's body. The skins were applied to the frames in the jig and countersunk riveted to the assembled frames. The rivets had to go through a heat treatment process to soften them and be used within two hours or they began to harden. Once the skin had been applied, the completed fuselage would have been removed from the jig and the long process of installing the internal equipment begun. The K5054's trials were a success and Supermarine received an initial Government production contract for 310 aircraft, with a second shortly after for 1,000. They would count towards a new British rearmament plan.

There has been much discussion about the origins of the Spitfire name. Sir Robert McLean, chairman of Supermarine and a director of Vickers-Armstrongs, which had bought Supermarine, wanted to call the F7/30 Type 224 the Spitfire, as he used to refer to his daughter as a 'little spitfire'. A letter was sent to the Air Ministry asking if they would reserve the name for the planned fighter but the Ministry replied: 'Until accepted for supply to the RAF, you will continue to refer to this aircraft as the Supermarine F7/30.' When the prototype 224 was taken on charge at Farnborough many months later, however, the service history carried the name Spitfire. When Mitchell's redesign of the F7/30 appeared as the Type 300, the name remained and a legend was made.

WE SAW IT BURN: TESTIMONY FROM INSIDE THE FIRESTORM

BY DAVID KEY

For Joan Tagg in Supermarine's accounts department on the fourth floor of the Woolston works, 23 August 1940 had been a busy but peaceful day. That was until the evening when, after dinner, the air raid sirens began to wail as the Luftwaffe started its evening attack of the city. Running for the public air raid shelters, she would be caught in the open as the bombs began to land.

Joan recalled in her diary:

> Each time we heard the whistle of a bomb, we threw ourselves down beside the railway bank, then ran on and fell down again each time we heard a bomb falling. Someone shouted: 'They're machine gunning,' so we didn't wait to find out but quickened our pace even more. When we finally reached the shelter our legs and arms were stinging – not machine gun bullets, but the result of falling in stinging nettles on the railway bank. We had not noticed them at the time, but once inside the shelter we suffered. As we looked out we saw German planes having fun shooting at the barrage balloons, which then came down in flames.[13]

By 7.45 that evening three more had passed over Southampton. 'I must admit that I am getting rather jittery, being constantly on the alert and am also feeling the effects of disturbed nights,' Joan confessed. 'Even though planes may not be overhead we do hear gunfire and are constantly up and down to the shelter.'

It was on 23 August that Joan learned of a development that would have profound implications for those on the factory floor. Workers were to remain at their posts and only allowed to leave when danger was considered 'imminent'. There was at that time a growing feeling among some in Government that aircraft production was suffering severely from interruptions due to air raid warnings and evacuations. Whatever the risk to the workforce, production had to be maintained and it seems that Supermarine had made the decision that its workers should not evacuate until the last possible moment. 'This means that we shall have even more perilous gallops to the shelters having come down several flights of stairs from the fourth floor,' Joan wrote.

That decision would have profound implications as the Luftwaffe increased its raids on the Supermarine works and the whole of Southampton. On 15 and 24 September, little or no warning was given and the bombs were already falling as workers attempted to reach the company's above-ground air raid shelters. On the 15th, Phil Pearce, a sheet metal worker who'd just turned 18, recalls diving for cover inside the factory before summoning the courage during a pause to make a dash for Supermarine's shelters on the nearby Peartree Common:

I remember hearing the sirens and almost instantaneously the ground shaking and I heard loud explosions, and I saw a very large press which I felt would give me more protection, so I quickly crawled under it as there was no way we could risk leaving the building with the bombing already under way.

Another worker joined me under the bench and during a lull in the attack we plucked up the courage to make a dash for the shelters. As we were now in the open, we quickly searched for some form of shelter and we could only find a small section of beach alongside the river between our factory and the next building, so we laid down there. Soon after, I heard an aircraft and looking up saw a German bomber flying very low over the river and the next thing I knew the shingle on the beach was flying up around me and I could see the rear gunner as he was strafing the area. It was nothing short of a miracle that we escaped unharmed, for the second time that day.

Britain was prepared for massive aerial bombardment, as the Nazis sought to destroy cities and manufacturing to break morale and the ability to fight back.

Large frames called jigs, crucial to Spitfire construction, were rescued from Woolston and Itchen and installed at the secret factory sites.

Phil was lucky not to have made it to either the shelter or the tunnel in the railway embankment that served as a cut-through to Peartree Common, as both took direct hits resulting in loss of life. 'We were shocked to see that the railway tunnel had received a direct hit and all that was left was a heap of rubble. We later learned that many of our co-workers who were in the shelters had been killed – so fate had meant we had survived,' he recalls.

Among those lost was Gilbert Olsen, a foreman in the jig and tool design department, who had been helping prepare Seward Garage on the Winchester Road in Shirley for fuselage production. From the roof of Seward's, Gilbert's colleagues watched the attack unfurl, unaware their boss was in the eye of the storm. His nephew, Peter Lucas, a child of 8 at the time, recalled: 'My uncle Gilbert ... who was at home, needed some paperwork, went back and got caught. I think he was killed by a blast under the bridge. I remember seeing the shelters there with direct hits.'

Denis Le Penn Webb, in the Supermarine Woolston works, later recalls scrambling over the railway embankment to see if there was anything he could do:

I could see the full tragedy. The bombs had missed the target of the works as usual and instead had landed on some of the shelters, which, in one case, had turned into a heap of soil and sand with arms and legs sticking out. Rescuers were already desperately digging in the hope that some people might get out alive.

The Luftwaffe returned at 4.30 on 26 September. Peter again recalls: 'We walked through the station cut, lovely day as I remember. We got to the top of Station Hill, heard the roar of engines, looked up and the blue patch of sky was full of bombers going over for another shot.' More than sixty bombers with fighter escorts hit the Itchen and Woolston works, along with the gas works and docks on the other side of the river. One riveter, 'Dinks' Diaper, recalled:

> There was hardly any time between when the air raid siren sounded and the bombs started falling. I came running out of the factory's F-Shop onto Hazel Road. Then up Sea Road under the brick railway arch. The resident publican of the Red Lion would leave the cellar doors open on the forecourt and I dived down into it for shelter.

The raid came only a matter of weeks after wages clerk Ellie Dewey had joined Supermarine. Forced to wait to leave the factory because of the bottleneck of workers in the doorway attempting to escape, she reached Hazel Road as the bombs were already falling. Diving for cover, a male colleague threw himself on her to protect her. Ellie's next memory was sitting in one of the long air raid shelters as dead and wounded workers were brought in. She was fortunate. For many others, caught in the open en route to the shelters, the railway arch Dinks had run under on Sea Road offered the prospect of safe cover. Sadly the arch was to prove no protection whatsoever and at least six were killed trying to shelter from the falling bombs.

The supposed elimination of the Spitfire factories wasn't the end of Southampton's suffering. Even though the Luftwaffe – as far as it was concerned – had put Spitfire production in the city out of business, its aircraft would strike Southampton repeatedly afterwards, peaking at the end of November with raids of up to seven hours in duration and consisting of up to 120 bombers. They took out the city's telephone exchange and destroyed water mains and gas supplies. With fire crews diminished by fatalities, exhaustion or injury, fire-fighting reserves were called in from seventy-five other districts as far away as Nottingham when bombers returned on 1 December. Despite this, many homes were simply left to burn to conserve water. In the words of one local resident who was referring to another British city pummelled by Nazi bombs, Southampton had been 'Coventrated'. The great port had been hit to such an extent that, by 2 December, a large part of the city centre had vanished. Nothing remained that was not 'wilted, wasted or warped'.[14]

It would take weeks before water, along with gas supplies, could be restored. Meantime, there was the human toll to consider. One hundred and thirty-seven people had perished, with many more injured, in just two successive nights of raids during November, and such was the psychological impact that many residents trekked out of the city at night to try and sleep elsewhere rather than chance being caught beneath another nocturnal firestorm. On his visits into the city, the Bishop of Winchester, Dr Garbett, said morale had collapsed. He recorded what he saw on the faces and in the body language of those he encountered. 'I went from parish to parish, and everywhere there was fear,'[15] he noted.

SECRET SAVIOUR OF THE SPITFIRE

It was Lord Beaverbrook who ordered the dispersal of the Spitfire factories and Supermarine's new works manager, Len Gooch, who oversaw their relocation and set-up, later receiving an OBE for his services. But the foundations for dispersal were laid by Gooch's predecessor, Supermarine works manager Hartley Blyth Pratt, better known as H.B. Pratt. Realising what bombing of the Southampton factories would mean for the Spitfire, Supermarine engaged Pratt, who'd already helped turn around struggling production, to come up with a plan for decentralised manufacturing to help safeguard supplies of Spitfires. Under Beaverbrook, and with the authority of the Ministry of Aircraft Production behind him, Gooch expanded Pratt's concept. Sadly, Pratt would not live to see the fruits of this idea realised at scale.

Pratt was a long-serving and visionary member of staff at expansionist engineering firm Vickers-Armstrongs, which had moved into weapons and armaments. His career with the company pre-dated the First World War, working initially on armaments but returning to focus on airships following a brief period in ship design on the Isle of Wight. It was thanks to Pratt that the legendary Barnes Wallis joined Vickers. Pratt developed a strong personal and working relationship with Wallis on ship design during this time and took him to Vickers, where they jointly worked on airships.

Pratt was a firm believer in the potential of the airship and, with Wallis, designed one of Britain's first rigid vessels and filed at least one patent on construction. Pratt saw a bright future for airships as luxury cruisers capable of carrying up to 100 passengers per flight and in 1919 outlined plans for a large commercial fleet. Vickers created an airship subsidiary employing Wallis to design bigger and more refined vessels as the Government explored the idea of an airship service for the Empire. The service never materialised but Wallis became a major figure in design at Vickers, conceiving the durable geodetic structure of the Wellington bomber and famously developing specialised ordnance that included the bouncing bombs used by RAF Lancasters on the German dams of the Ruhr Valley in May 1943. Pratt's future lay in a different direction – as the Spitfire's secret saviour.

Vickers Aviation bought Supermarine Aviation Works on the strength of the emerging talents of R.J. Mitchell and his Schneider Trophy-winning racing planes, but recognised that sea-racing planes alone were not enough to make money. The small maker of wooden floatplanes based on the banks of the Solent therefore had to modernise, so the armaments giant brought in one of its own men to reorganise, rationalise and expand production. The changes, however, were not complete by the time the Air Ministry placed its first orders for Spitfires. A shortage of floor space and skilled workers meant orders were not delivered on time. Initial hold-ups were also caused by problems with supplies of Spitfire wing sub-assemblies, with the contractors blaming the poor standard of drawings supplied by Supermarine and Supermarine suggesting subcontractors had failed to get in direct contact with its drawing office to resolve issues.

Things weren't helped in Southampton when Vickers reassigned the individual who'd been leading the reorganisation to another factory. As Spitfire production lagged, so did the RAF's rearmament, with Supermarine incurring the wrath of the increasingly frantic Government. Vickers brought in Pratt as works manager at the end of 1937. He duly completed the reorganisation and rationalisation and succeeded in bringing Spitfire production back on target by March 1939. Supermarine's legendary test pilot, Jeffrey Quill, would describe Pratt as 'a calm, methodological and unexcitable man who applied all those qualities to recovering the situation',[16] despite bearing the brunt of outside anger for Supermarine's failure to deliver as promised.

Pratt's next act was to draw up a plan for the survival of Spitfire production should the Woolston and Itchen factories be knocked out. If there was a fault in Pratt's thinking, it was that he didn't plan big enough – or act fast enough. Alarm bells about the vulnerability of Supermarine's Southampton factories had been triggered by early Luftwaffe flights over the city. Pratt picked a handful of locations across Southampton that included garages and factories, but the Spitfire production equipment did not begin to move out in anticipation of potential attacks. Relocation only started in the wake of the 15 September raid, after which Pratt began the hunt for a second tranche of sites suitable for conversion to Spitfire factories – taking the total to twenty-seven.

It took the Luftwaffe's raid of 26 September to dramatically escalate Pratt's plan, but sadly, he would not be in the driving seat. Wounded like many of his colleagues during the firestorm of 24 September, Pratt had also been badly traumatised by the scenes of carnage he witnessed. With the Woolston and Itchen plants smouldering after 26 September and Pratt both physically injured and mentally scarred, the responsibility fell to Gooch to initiate dispersal on a grand scale. As the design team relocated in December to Hursley Park, Hampshire, and with a new management team taking over, Pratt would be removed from his role. Overworked and suffering depression, the quiet saviour of the Spitfire took his own life not long afterwards.

2

PEOPLE AND PLACES OF THE SECRET FACTORIES

Approximately 23 miles (37km) to the north of Southampton lies Salisbury. Nestled in the heart of Wiltshire and known as the city in the countryside, Salisbury lacks the busy feel of its urban neighbour with its large and industrialised waterfront. Rather, Salisbury sits astride the picturesque River Avon, its roads and ambling lanes studded with low-slung, half-timbered Tudor buildings. Surveying everything from above is the famous 403ft (123m) spire of its jewel of a medieval cathedral, home to a copy of Magna Carta. Not far from the city lies Salisbury Plain and the mysterious, ancient stone circle of Stonehenge.

During the Second World War, however, this calm and serene exterior hid an unprecedented experiment in British military and industrial production that turned the city into one of the largest centres of secret Spitfire production, delivering more than 2,000 of the iconic aircraft. It was an experiment that would see these Spitfires built inside a range of small factories, businesses and other high street locations adapted for purpose. Salisbury was the first in an eventual network of cities and towns across the south of England picked for Spitfire production after the Luftwaffe's bombing of Southampton.

Like everywhere else, however, the obvious sources of labour had been squeezed dry by the war. Men of fighting age – legally defined as between 18 and 41 – had been drafted into the military, meaning men who'd worked in industry before the war and who might have switched to making Spitfires were simply not available. The burden therefore fell upon women and from early 1941 all women aged 18 to 60 had to register for so-called war work. Conscription followed in December, when unmarried women considered 'mobile' and aged 20 to 30 were offered the option of working in industry or joining the women's branches of one of the armed services. The timing couldn't have been better for Supermarine as it took over its first covert factories.

Among those jobs considered war work was manufacturing, meaning that thousands of women could be assigned to the secret Spitfire factories in Salisbury, Reading and Trowbridge. They worked alongside retired men and boys too young to fight. One such person was Bette Blackwell. Just turned 20 and born and raised 6 miles outside Salisbury in the village of Downton, Bette had worked as a hairdresser at the war's start. She was called up for interview and underwent a medical to determine a suitable line of war work. Having passed the medical, Bette was told to report to Wessex Motor Garage, New Street, as a riveter. Wessex Garage specialised in fuselages, tail units and wing leading edges – the smooth section of wing that helped determine air flow and so helped contribute to the plane's responsiveness.

Like many a local civilian, Bette had no idea Wessex Motors had ceased to work on vehicles and was now secretly building Spitfires:

> I had notification from the Government and we had to report to this place in Salisbury for medical examination, and from there we were told to go to this other place, which was the Wessex Motor Garage and I can remember saying: 'Why have we got to go there, we don't know nothing about cars' ... And we went into this place and the noise, it was terrific. All you got was brrr, brrr, brrr. We couldn't hear one another speak, we were shouting at the top of our voices. And I was introduced to a man who was the chargehand, and he told me apparently that I'd passed the exam to be a riveter.

Stan Gordon was another secret factory worker in Salisbury. Stan grew up in Orchard Road, Bemerton, left school at 14 and two years later found himself assigned to the Witt and Vincent Garage, Devizes Road, which had been turned over to Spitfire production. Today it's back to its former use. 'We had a mixed bag of labour there, mostly ladies of various ages and, as you can probably imagine, at the age of 17 it forwarded my education quite considerably,' Stan reflects.

Joan Johns, 18 at the time, was sent to work testing piston rings at Wellworthy Piston Rings, which was part of the secret network supplying parts. A grammar school graduate, Joan's short career history to that point had been very white collar, having followed shorthand training to work as a typist in a bank. 'It was a very big factory, mind you I saw very little of the factory floor because I was upstairs working in the laboratory testing piston rings,' Joan says of Wellworthy's. Joyce Hunt, then also 18, was sent to the Hilperton Road Factory, Trowbridge. 'They asked you: "Would you like to be a land girl, or in the air force?" and I said:

Vincents Garage, which manufactured Spitfire sub assemblies in busy Reading, had occupied this spot close to the station.

Vincents Garage, with its imposing exterior, was almost opposite the busy Reading Station yet operated in total secrecy.

Inside, Vincents ran a massive operation building Spitfire fuselages and sub-assemblies.

"No, I couldn't milk a cow!" And I said to my mate: "What shall we do, Phyl?" and she said: "We'll go in the Spitfire factory," and so we did.'

Pat Pearce was given a choice between joining the forces or the Women's Land Army. Pat's working life had followed a path not uncommon to many women who'd work at these factories: service in one of the big, local houses and as a shop assistant – at Woolworths and Marks and Spencer – before being called up. She was assigned to the Wilts and Dorset Bus Company in Salisbury. Recalling the enormous size and scale of what was a clandestine operation, Pat says:

I shall never forget the day I started. It was frightening really. There were all these people, ready to start on their jobs and we were right over the other side and we all had different little jobs. But then it got so noisy you could hardly hear yourself speak!

Betty Potter had volunteered for the Women's Royal Air Force (WRAF) but fate took her to Bradley Road, Trowbridge, instead. 'We volunteered for the WRAF and they said they'd let us know, but they never did. We were 19 so we just had to go into the factory. Best thing we ever did, actually – it was wonderful!'

'I shall never forget the day I started. It was frightening really,' says Pat, fourth from left. 'It got so noisy you could hardly hear yourself speak!'

Not everybody working at these secret locations came from close by, and some were assigned to places sufficiently distant that they'd never been there before. Betty was one such person – someone who'd worked in domestic service at a big house in her village after school. 'We were 11 miles from Devizes and 15 miles from Salisbury so there was no work there – there was no choice other than going into service in the big houses,' she says. 'Living 20 miles away we'd never even heard of Trowbridge.'

Others were from even further afield. These were a relatively small category whose skills or knowledge made them of particular value to Supermarine. One of these was artist draughtswoman Stella Rutter, who at the outbreak of war worked as a tracer for the Royal Navy in Portsmouth 40 miles (64km) away. In this era before documents could be reproduced electronically, engineering organisations relied on those who could trace original designs to produce copies that would then be used by others in design or assembly.

Tracers were a vital cog in the engineering design process; people with the attention to detail, drawing and engineering skills to reproduce designs accurately and to spot and correct any mistakes. Without them, machines such as Spitfires could not make the leap from drawing board to battlefield. A chance meeting between her father and Gerald Gingell, the influential leader of Supermarine's technical publications department, would lead to Stella being snapped up by Supermarine and promoted. She joined the drawing, design and planning offices, which had moved to the magnificent 350-acre estate of Hursley Park in December 1940.

One of the few women, Stella was working in an office that grew to more than 150 draughtsmen and tracers. She made ink-drawn master copies of assembly drawings produced by her team. Once completed, these drawings would be printed for distribution to the factories, to help workers assemble the Spitfires. Stella worked with the top echelons of the company including Gingell, Lovell Cooper, and Joe Smith, who became chief designer sometime after the death of R.J. Mitchell. Her team comprised three artist draughtsmen and no less a figure than Gingell himself. Twenty-year-old Stella was the only woman. 'I was commandeered from my job in Portsmouth with the Navy for this

Bette Blackwell at 20: assigned to riveting at Salisbury's Wessex Motors.

particular job because I was the only one who had the skills to do it ... In those days, women never did draughtsmanship but I had those skills,' Stella says.

The centre of Spitfire production in Salisbury was four units on Castle Street: two close together belonging to the Wilts and Dorset Bus Company, a factory unit backing onto that, and the Anna Valley Motor Garage. Despite their central locations, these factories operated in almost complete secrecy. Partially assembled Spitfires could pass through large doors and be taken by lorry to a nearby airfield for final assembly. These doors onto the street might be open during the night but were firmly closed at dawn and remained shut during daylight hours for fear of drawing attention and unwanted questions.

Once a fuselage had been made there was a lot of work fitting out. To cater for this in Salisbury, Supermarine built Spitfire Factory No. 1 on a stretch of land on Castle Road that was close to the Iron Age fort and medieval settlement of Old Sarum. Here, final assembly was conducted on the fuselage with the engine added before being sent to an airfield at High Post for final assembly, flight test and dispatch to RAF maintenance units. A second factory was built a year later below the site of Factory No. 1, responsible for leading edges and wings. Factory No. 2 remains today – a long, low, corrugated, shed-like building with sloping roof fronted by a white and blue facade. The first factory has gone, its floor now the site of a car park.

Top to bottom: Castle Street – here today – housed three Spitfire factories; inside one of the three Wilts and Dorset Bus facilities that was big enough for wing construction; the exterior of the Omnibus unit today that was responsible for fuselage production, wing leading edges and tail sections.

Top to bottom: huge concertina doors, normally closed to maintain secrecy, open in this contemporary sketch for the transport of completed sub assemblies; one former site of the bus company's operations; the Wilts and Dorset units were a hive of activity.

Some 50 miles (80km) away to the north-east, the Spitfire production units at Reading were also being established. And just like all the other dispersal sites, the factories were never obvious. One prime site in Reading was Vincents Garage, a large, stout, stone building on a roundabout almost opposite Reading Station, a busy mainline hub connecting London to the South, South-West and Midlands. Gone now – replaced by red-brick offices – Vincents had been a car and coach engineering and repair works when Supermarine moved in.

Reading boy Peter Smith walked past Vincents Garage every day, oblivious to the Spitfire operation inside.

A feature of this then hard-to-miss building was a grand main entrance flanked by columns and large windows that were either covered or filled with displays. What lay inside would have put passers-by in a tail spin: construction of Spitfire fuselages, detailing and sub-assembly. Peter Smith, a young boy at the time, recalled being completely unaware of the existence of this manufacturing hotspot in the middle of busy Reading. Peter tells us:

> I used to walk with mother into Reading to do shopping, and we walked past the station past a place called Vincents. And it didn't strike me at the time, but there was nothing going on there, there was just a glass shopfront where they had one or two cars and various other displays. It wasn't until recently that I realised just what went on at Vincents.

The garage was one of five sites in the Reading area working together. Another local site requisitioned was Great Western Motors, Vastern Road, which would become responsible for all the Spitfire wings produced in the Reading factory system. Wings were taken to a specially built factory in Caversham Road, where they would be finished. Fuselages were brought up from Vincents Garage and all components were taken up to an airfield at Henley, 8 miles outside Reading, for final assembly and flight tests. The Spitfires, however, would outgrow Henley and in due course the operation was moved to RAF Aldermaston, where a special hangar was built. Following flight testing, the now-complete aircraft would be handed over to the civilian pilots of the Air Transport Auxiliary (ATA), who would fly them to the waiting RAF.

The main centres of Spitfire production – Salisbury, Reading, Trowbridge and Southampton – were supplied by parts from a network of independent businesses or smaller, specialist units or workshops that could operate on a surprisingly small scale. Newbury was home to six units feeding the Reading factories but even right in the middle of Reading there were small units tucked away among the houses. One of the smallest workshops was actually in Peter's house: his father had a lathe set up in the spare bedroom, from where he made parts for aircraft fuel lines from magnesium alloy.

Peter recalled:

Father was always busy doing something and I hadn't realised it but in 1941 he was asked to make parts for the war effort. The first time that I realised something was going on in the house was when my father and a couple of burly gentlemen were taking parts of a big lathe up to the back bedroom, because that's where he was going to set it up and make parts for the war effort, although I didn't really understand that at the time.

Peter's father would prove industrious and resourceful – adapting to circumstances as the war developed. He would later take on more lathes and relocated the workshop from the spare bedroom to the family's kitchen when the bedroom was needed for evacuees.

Peter recalls of his father's skill:

He had acquired a German watchmaker's lathe, but all the feed threads were the opposite hand to any other lathes, so when you wanted to move the tool away from the workpiece you had to turn it clockwise. There was no way my father could retrain himself for the functions he wanted to perform, so he got an old treadle sewing machine, took the sewing machine off, mounted the lathes on top of this cast iron and wooden base, and there was this 5-horsepower motor he put in the bottom with an open belt that ran up to the belt and pulley system in the headstock of the lathe. He modified it to make it so you could do several operations without taking the workpiece out. He made the tool post like a capstan so it could rotate and you could get a different angle on things. I used to spend quite a few afternoons in the top room listening.

Peter's mother became involved, too. 'He taught my mother and it didn't seem to take him or my mother that long to learn how to make screws. She was making thousands and thousands of them,' Peter says.

The third dispersal centre was Trowbridge, which opened in 1940 but began its own production line in 1943. After the factories in Salisbury and Reading had become established, a purpose-built factory was constructed at Bradley Road. This was supported by another new unit in Hilperton Road, where wings were built and sub-assembly undertaken. This also acted as a storage facility for tools. As with all the other centres, an airfield was required. Hidden behind the quiet village of Steeple Ashton was Keevil Airfield, which was used for the final assembly and dispersal of the aircraft. As well as satellite workshops in surrounding towns such as Hungerford and Westbury, there were small units scattered across the centre of Trowbridge, behind various facades that hid the work from the public. These units were responsible for producing parts for the main factory, with two such units based at what was then the Fore Street Garage and the Central Garage that made skins for wings.

Immediately following the Luftwaffe raid on 15 September, Supermarine had activated the Southampton-based dispersal plan masterminded by works manager H.B. Pratt, with equipment and production moved to Hendy's Garage off Pound Tree Road and Seward Garage on the Winchester Road in Shirley. At the same time, more sites were requisitioned to scatter Spitfire works across the city. It was not long before production recovered, with more than 4,500 Spitfires built by the secret factories in Southampton. Again, an airfield was required for final assembly of the aircraft built in Southampton. Eastleigh was the destination for all the sections, with the sub-assemblies integrated, tested and flown out to the RAF.

The incredible thing about the secret factories was that they would remain such well-guarded secrets despite their considerable size and the large-scale nature of their work. Set in garages, factories and bus depots on main roads and side streets, it was their very ordinariness that helped to conceal them among houses and commercial premises. Although off limits to civilians, one person who did

As a telegram boy, Gordon Topp got to see inside Spitfire factories, which he called 'a real eye opener'. 'The number of people who worked there to produce them – it was enormous!'

get a peek inside was a 14-year-old telegram messenger boy named Gordon Topp. Telegrams were messages sent electronically by wire between bureaus but delivered to the intended recipient as a printout on a card by a uniformed messenger. Telegrams were the responsibility of the Government-owned General Post Office, whose messengers would sign the Official Secrets Act. The Act was meant to guard against espionage and unauthorised disclosure of information to an enemy, and was used to shield vital sites such as the Spitfire factories.

Gordon was amazed by what he saw behind the everyday facade of factories such as Anna Valley Garage: they might have been unconventional and relatively small locations but the operations inside were on a par with any large-scale aircraft manufacturing process of the time. He tells us:

> When you went to these Spitfire factories, it was a real eye opener. The bodies of the Spitfires were all in line like you see in these American aircraft factories now and there were girls and they had trousers on and they were working on bodies with mainly older men that were too old to go into service and fight. The bodies were in lines – six bodies in each line – and the same with the wings, the wings were in line all up through the factory. It was quite amazing. And the number of people who worked there to produce them – it was enormous really, when you think about it.

Bette, at Salisbury's Wessex Garage on New Street, which produced Spitfire fuselages, tail units and leading edges, concurs as to the cloud of invisibility that seemed to envelop the factories. The secrecy was maintained even when it came to moving large sub-assemblies – units of fuselages or wing sections – out into the open for transport using specially built, low-loader lorries. Bette recalls:

> [The doors] were like a concertina and you would never have known what the whole area did, because there were things on the wall that made it look like a [solid] wall. You didn't know the doors opened for planes to come out ... I don't think anybody knew there was a Spitfire factory there.

These doors helped maintain the veil of secrecy.

> I worked there two or three years and in all that time I never saw an aircraft move out of the factory. One day we were coming back from the canteen, and along the road in front of us was this great big long thing and they said this was one of the aircraft – one at the front going out. When we got back to the factory they were closing the doors.

On two occasions special walls were built inside existing commercial buildings. One was the Barnes Steamroller plant in Southwick, Trowbridge, which saw 75 per cent of the floor space assigned to Spitfire production and the remainder given over to the pre-wartime business of building steamrollers. Another was at the Wilts and Dorset, whose buildings had plenty of free space and high ceilings for Pat and others working in shifts around the clock to produce Spitfire wings but where buses continued to trundle in and out. In both cases, brick walls were thrown up to keep the operations separate and help ensure anonymity and security for the Spitfires.

Resident John Bletsoe says the residents living in close proximity to these neighbourhood factories had little idea as to the true nature of their business:

> We thought that they repaired Spitfires. We'd seen them coming on these low-loaders with the wings folded and thought they were going in for repair. I didn't realise that they were going to be fitted out. And we were told they were repairing them – had no idea they were building them. No idea at all – and I lived three minutes' walk away!

Doreen Andrews was five when the war broke out and lived in a house on Castle Street opposite the Wilts and Dorset in Salisbury, where Pat Pearce and colleagues were busy building Spitfire wings. Even with two family connections to this factory, she was completely unaware of the round-the-clock wartime operation running

Doreen Andrews lived opposite the bus garage on Castle Street, Salisbury, but was unaware of the Spitfire operation, even though her auntie Winnie was one of the workers.

opposite. Her father was a member of the Home Guard volunteer force dedicated to duties such as the defence of key installations including factories, as well as being a fire watcher. Operating in shifts and keeping watch from high up on the roofs, fire watchers would respond to German incendiary bombs, attempting to extinguish or contain the blaze until the fire brigade arrived. Initially a voluntary duty, fire watching became compulsory as the Blitz took hold and fire watchers armed with stirrup pumps, buckets of water and sandbags were deployed at factories and other vital sites. The authorities were eager to avoid a repeat of Southampton, so fire watchers in Salisbury would have been under instruction to watch over buildings like the Wilts and Dorset. Doreen's dad never let on why he might have been looking after something as seemingly innocuous and relatively unimportant to the war effort as a bus garage in Salisbury. 'I remember dad standing up on the roof with a bucket and a pump on his fire watch and we'd ask: "What you doing, dad?" and he'd say: "Watching the Wiltshire and Dorset." So thinking back, he knew what was in the depot.'

Doreen's aunt Winnie, meanwhile, was among the stream of workers entering and leaving this busy building each day and yet a connection to the war effort and to Spitfires was not made:

Early in the morning, my auntie Winnie was one of them, and she used to pop in and say 'hello' before she went to work. We saw these people go in and we still thought they were making buses ... Nobody told you. It was a secret. I think if one person had told, then the wrong person would have heard. 'The walls have ears,' as they used to say.

Such was the degree of secrecy and discipline in not discussing the work that the precise scale – and even existence – of these factories was sometimes not apparent even to those involved. Joan at Wellworthy's was incredulous that she was part of such a huge – and hidden – system of mass production. 'It wasn't until after the war that I realised how extensive Salisbury was for the making of Spitfire parts, and how they were all assembled and flown off from the sheds at High Post,' she says. The secret was maintained within the Wilts and Dorset itself. Working for a while on buses inside that partitioned space was local boy Roy Fittall. According to Roy, nobody knew the type of aircraft being built on the other side of the dividing wall. 'It was all shuttered up,' Roy says.

High Post was one of two sites in the Salisbury area used for final assembly of Spitfires, flight testing and dispatch to RAF units by the ATA. High Post lies about 4 miles outside Salisbury city centre and was home to the High Post Aerodrome Hotel, built around 1936 in the contemporary art deco style, not unlike the extension to Supermarine's Woolston factory in Southampton. It was the very modern clubhouse of the Wiltshire Flying School. The location was perfect, set deep in the countryside with a convenient local landmark, the Amesbury All Electric Petrol Station, a gingerbread-house-style brick building with a sloping roof that offered the first all-electric power pump, a public phone and attendant service. An outpost of the future in the farmlands of Wiltshire, petrol attendants stood ready to fill the tanks of the few cars and motorcycles speeding along this remote part of the A345.

But all was not what it seemed and these thoroughly modern service buildings and the surrounding fields masked a valuable military secret. Nestled behind the petrol station and obscured by the hotel lay facilities that played a vital role in the delivery of the secret Spitfires. The flying club's airfield had been turned over to the final assembly of Spitfires and had been upgraded to support testing of new variants rolling off the designers' drawing boards. High Post was served by three runways – one parallel to the A345 – with one extended to cater for the later models of the more advanced and heavier aircraft that evolved as the war progressed. Purpose-built hangars were used to house and assemble lots of aeroplanes at the same time with an experimental unit established for development, complete with a drawing office and engineering team.

Part of the Spitfire's success in the arms race against the Luftwaffe came from the adaptability its designer R.J. Mitchell had built in – an adaptability that would ensure the Spitfire became the longest-serving continuously modified plane of the Second World War. The twenty-four marques of Spitfire that would eventually emerge from Hursley offered, among other things, improved performance at different altitudes, with a branch of the family – known as the Seafire – built for use on Royal Navy aircraft carriers. During the war, experimental centres such as these were critical to the race to develop the superior fighting plane.

The hotel and petrol services at High Post remain today, but transformed into something more mundane: a low-rise, red-brick hotel has superseded its art deco predecessor and the All Electric has been replaced by a modern forecourt-style service station. You could be on a country A-road anywhere in present-day Britain, but Spitfire historian and former Vickers Supermarine engineer Norman Parker vividly recalls High Post in its prime:

> What used to happen was the pieces of the aircraft, the fuselage, wings and so on, were brought up on the lorry from Salisbury and they would be taken into the hangar through a little bit of the modern building, through a large doorway. Component parts were taken in, assembled, tested, taken out onto the airfield and flown out to the RAF maintenance units.

The Spitfire hangars are gone and nature is closing in, but the woods at Chattis Hill today are a testament to where they once stood.

As the war progressed and Spitfires became heavier and more powerful, longer runways were required so Supermarine closed the nearby Woodford Valley Road and built a grass runway across it to provide the additional length.

About 12 miles to the east of Salisbury was another location, and – as with High Post – it was an airfield with factories hidden deep in the countryside. An unassuming small track off the A30 now aptly named Spitfire Lane leads to what was a major manufacturing and distribution site for Spitfires, at Chattis Hill. Then, as now, Chattis Hill from above resembled a nearly triangular-shaped copse of mature trees (now named Spitfire Wood) at the intersection of a patchwork of vast fields and connecting hedgerows. When the site was taken over in December 1940, it was decided to build two corrugated, T2 hangars and use the surrounding trees as camouflage. A number of trees were cut down to make way for the hangars' floor of 31,350 sq ft (2,912 sq m), with the remainder close by pulled back using ropes during construction and then released upon completion.

Spitfires would be collected from Chattis, as from the other airfields in the secret network, by the pilots of the ATA. The ATA was a unique force in British aviation history, a civilian operation with a strong core of women pilots whose job it was to ferry warplanes great and small from factory and repair bases around the nation to RAF and American air bases across Britain, saving fighter pilots the task. Among the ATA's ranks was Mary Wilkins-Ellis, who still recalls the effectiveness of the natural wooded camouflage at Chattis that you might usually expect to find in the thick forests of Europe or Asia, not in the fields of England. 'I went to Chattis many, many

As you were: Chattis Hill's then new hangars in 1940 were set among the trees to provide cover from the enemy and allow work on Spitfires to continue unnoticed.

times,' she tells us 'and having got there, the Spitfires were all ready for us. But the factory was in among the woods, so you couldn't see it.'

Supermarine was not the only aircraft maker in Britain to be specifically targeted by the Luftwaffe and nor was it the first to relocate. Stirling bomber manufacturer Short Bros moved production out of its base in Rochester, Kent, to other parts of the country following a Luftwaffe raid during the Battle of Britain that destroyed factories and aircraft, setting back production by at least a year. Short Bros eventually concentrated its production in Belfast, considered out of reach of enemy aircraft. Supermarine chose not to simply set up shop in new, large-scale factories elsewhere: such was the perceived importance of the Spitfire, the firm was determined to avoid any future interruption to supply by sending its factories underground.

In this, Supermarine not only successfully moved its large and centralised manufacturing to a set of distributed, small locations but it did so without arousing public attention. In a testament to the brilliance of both the idea and execution, the first secret Spitfire was delivered just over six months after the Southampton raids, with the secret network powering up to eventually produce around half of all Spitfires. Further, the system was slick enough to absorb change and cope with the rapid pace of new designs intended to push the Spitfire further in the arms race against the Luftwaffe.

The muscle behind this success was provided by the men, boys and record numbers of women overlooked in peacetime but mobilised through the necessity of war. The recruits of this shadow army had been entrusted the vital task of building what the Government had determined would be one of its most important assets in the war. Delivering on that challenge would see local populations of shop assistants and domestic workers, who would otherwise not have been considered for such work, turn themselves into a crack force of skilled engineers and fitters. Working long hours in difficult and demanding conditions, Supermarine's ghost army would evolve.

BY THE NUMBERS: SECRET FACTORIES' FACTS AND FIGURES

BY NORMAN PARKER

Nothing like it had been attempted before: the break-up and dispersal of a highly centralised, wartime manufacturing operation, with activities packed into a range of smaller units and manufacturing successfully resumed. Yet that's what Supermarine achieved following the raids on Woolston and Itchen. With so many units operating across such a broad area, planning, communication and co-ordination were critical. In this set up, a template was rolled out in four areas, where hubs were fed by smaller facilities and served by airfields. A staggering number and variety of facilities were built or requisitioned and upgraded by Vickers Supermarine. 12,000 planes were manufactured with 8,000 traced so far using surviving company documents.

Southampton

Of the four dispersal areas, Southampton already had a number of additional units before the final bombing of late September 1940. The basic facts about the Southampton units are known, but many details were lost or simply not set down.

Before the bombing 24/26 September 1940

Name	Function	Floor area	Opened	Closed
Itchen Works	Production, Spitfire, Sea Otter	80,400 sq ft	2-38	27-9-40
Woolston Works	Production & experimental	150,000 sq ft	1912	27-9-40
Itchen Works site	Requisitioned by Royal Navy for storage of undersea pipeline	---	29-10-43	---
Eastleigh Airport	Assembly, flight test	144,400 sq ft	1-9-32	31-12-57

Weston Rolling Mills	Tanks and pipes	24,000 sq ft	23-11-39	30-4-46
Seawards Garage	Toolmakers, jigs & templates	25,000 sq ft	10-9-40	30-11-46
Hampshire & Dorset Bus Garage	Wings	18,706 sq ft	19-9-40	30-4-46
Hendy's Garage	Fuselages & tanks	24,720 sq ft	31-12-39	31-12-45
Lowther's Garage	Machine shop & toolroom	7,713 sq ft	1-12-40	31-10-46
Deepdene House	Accounts & commercial office	5,000 sq ft	11-39	2-8-44

Total floor area 458,339 sq ft

After the bombing 24/26 September 1940

Name	Function	Floor area	Opened	Closed
Polygon Hotel	Works management & admin staff	4th floor	<29-9-40	30-11-40
Southampton College outbuildings	Design office	Unknown	29-9-40	1-12-40
Hollybrook Stores	Storage	7,700 sq ft	30-9-40	1-5-44
Holt House	Aeronautical inspection directorate & office for inspection	1,600 sq ft	27-11-40	29-12-45
Sunlight Laundry	Details & sub-assemblies	20,000 sq ft	<30-11-40	28-2-45
Austin House Garage	Tank coverage & training	9,000 sq ft	19-10-40	15-10-45
Chisnel's Garage, Winchester	Press shop & sheet metal detailing	9,000 sq ft	<30-11-40	31-03-47
Short's Garage	Machine shop	16,876 sq ft	<30-11-40	30-9-46
Hursley Park House	Main office	85,000 sq ft	30-11-40	24-6-54
	Experimental dept hangar & workshops	5,000 sq ft	<30-11-40	24-6-58

	Drawing office	27,420 sq ft	6-42	24-6-58
	Robin hangars	3,188 sq ft	1-41	24-6-58
	Gardener's bothy	Unknown	31-12-42	Unknown
Southend House	Accounts	11,700 sq ft	30-9-48	30-9-48
RNAS Worthy Down	Assembly & experimental flying	15,500 sq ft	12-40	6-6-43
Garret's Garage, Chandler's Ford	Transport repairs	6,929 sq ft	10-12-40	30-10-45
Land at Garret's Garage	Transport	14,000 sq ft	1-41	30-10-45
Hendy's Garage, Chandler's Ford	Pre-production	16,388 sq ft	30-9-40	30-9-46
Marwell Wall, W. Botley Stores	Finished components	12,000 sq ft	14-1-42	30-11-47
Park Place, near Southampton	Rivet sorting by the Women's Voluntary Service	1,200 sq ft	1941	23-8-45
Sholing Store	Finished parts store	2,568 sq ft	1942	31-3-47
Botley Store	Finished parts store	5,000 sq ft	1942	30-11-45
Bishop's Waltham Store	Finished parts store	11,700 sq ft	1942	31-3-47
Sleepy Hollow Barn, Ampfield	Accounts records	11,700 sq ft	1942	30-9-47
Two sheds, 16 Wilton Road, Southampton	---	120,393 sq ft	18-6-43	---
Land, Wonston, Sutton Scotney	---	Unknown	2-2-42	---
Leigh Road Stores, Eastleigh (extended 1-6-43)	Stores	6,400 sq ft	<30-11-40	28-2-48
Land, Vincent's Walk	---	2,730 sq ft	---	---
Land, Saxone shoe shop	---	350 sq ft	---	---

Total floor area: 424,111 sq ft
Number of aircraft produced that can be traced: 4,360

Key:
Not all dates and figures were accurately recorded at the time. Where a date is prefixed with an < to indicate before, or where a date is either month/year or just year, this indicates an incomplete record. Where the amount of floor space is 'unknown' this is listed as such. Dash (-) is not applicable.

Reading

Reading and Salisbury were virgin sites, started from scratch. Reading production was centred around Vincents Garage, close to the railway station. The ornate facade of this building belied the industrial-scale space behind. Reading did have an engineering heritage from which a labour force could be sourced, although it was lacking in aeronautical skills.

Name	Function	Floor area	Opened	Closed
Stradling's Garage, Newbury	Detail fittings	16,000 sq ft	<30-11-40	31-10-45
Pass Garage, Newbury	Process department	7,020 sq ft	5-10-40	28-2-46
Nias Garage, Newbury	Toolmakers	4,000 sq ft	<30-11-40	5-3-48
Nias Garage, Newbury	Stores	3,600 sq ft	<30-11-40	5-3-48
Venture Bus Garage, Newbury	Stores	7,000 sq ft	19-5-42	18-10-44
Messer's Garage, Mill Lane, Newbury	Sub-assemblies	19,705 sq ft	1-42	5-3-48
Shaw Works, Newbury	Press & machine shop	83,396 sq ft	7-43	28-2-59

Hungerford Garage, Newbury	Machine shop	28,081sq ft	12-41	30-9-46
Vincents Garage, Reading	Fuselages, details	43,500sq ft	<30-11-40	28-2-46
Great Western Garage, Reading	Wings	23,470 sq ft	<30-11-40	30-11-45
Central Garage, Reading	Canteen	3,000 sq ft	1942	28-2-46
Caversham Factory, Reading	Fuselages, engine installation	18,703 sq ft	20-2-42	30-4-46
Henley Aerodrome	Final assembly, flight test	10,774 sq ft	5-5-41	10-1-44
Aldermaston	Final assembly, flight test	27,571 sq ft	7-43	20-7-46

Total floor area: 295,820 sq ft
Number of aircraft produced that can be traced: 757

Salisbury

Production was centred on the Wessex Motors Garage in New Street. Fuselage jigs were installed and the site used to first assemble and then fit out the structure with the necessary internal equipment. Wing jigs were installed at the Wilts and Dorset Bus Company in Castle Street, near the railway bridge. The Anna Valley Motor Garage, also in Castle Street, saw jigs installed for construction of the Spitfire's tail unit and wing leading edges, with the site also used to build engine cowlings, flying controls and small structures. A new factory was built in Hudson's Field in the shadow of Old Sarum Castle. Simply known as Factory No. 1, this was used to finish fuselage and engine assembly while Factory No. 2, built a year later, was used to build sub-assemblies. The area was served by two airfields, High Post Aerodrome and Chattis Hill, with an additional aerodrome opened on the gallops of Attee Persee's racing stables on Chattis Hill. Chattis Hill, on the A30 near Stockbridge, was taken over in December 1940 with the first aircraft flying out on 29 March 1941, and the last departing on 22 March 1945 – a Mk XIV, serial SM842, going to No. 6 Maintenance Unit. With the end of Spitfire production, Chattis Hill was turned over to storage before closing in 1948.

High Post, the pre-war home of the Wiltshire School of Flying located on the Salisbury–Amesbury Road, was taken over in February 1941. One of its two hangars was rebuilt from another at Stonehenge Aerodrome, which had been used for a First World War Handley Page bomber. The airfield had been extended in 1936 to include the newly built High Post Aerodrome Hotel. High Post's runways were perfectly capable of accommodating the early Spitfires, but had to be extended as the planes' power and weight increased and they needed longer take-off and landing strips. The road from High Post to Middle Woodford was closed off at the High Post end, using three Hawker Tomtit fuselages, and replaced with the concrete track that exists today down to Coffee Farm from the end of the 2,000ft grass runway along to Greater Durnford Road. The Ministry of Aircraft Production added two coupled Type B1 hangars alongside the main road as a new home for the Experimental Department, then lodging at RNAS Worthy Down.

High Post was also the base for the test pilots who flew out to other airfields as required. Many of these were service pilots resting between tours of combat who undertook routine testing of production aircraft. The hotel was used for accommodation, with six railway carriages brought in for further space, as well as an ablutions block alongside the Woodford road. There was also a gun-site for airfield protection. But they did not, initially, have a control tower. When the hotel was built in 1936, it had a glass cupola built into the roof, which people thought had been designed for air traffic control: in fact it originally housed neon tubes that flashed out the letters H and P in Morse code, an ingenious advertising device for the hotel that could be seen some 20 miles away. It became an air traffic control tower, complete with the addition of a staircase. As production came to an end in Salisbury, Chattis Hill became a storage site but High Post continued its experimental flying until it closed in February 1947 and moved to Chilbolton airfield in Hampshire.

As well as the Supermarine units building Spitfires in Salisbury, there was an additional industrial unit near Netherhampton just to the west of the city that was used to store completed Spitfire fuselages, although this is not recorded in the official list of buildings used.

Existing aerodromes and newly built airfields served as bases for final construction and dispersal, while Worthy Down, here, was also home to experimental work.

Some factories, such as the Barnes Brothers Steamroller Factory, were dedicated to one particular activity such as wing leading edges ...

... while others, including the Anna Valley Motor Garage on Castle Street, undertook a range of activities that included construction of tail units, engine cowlings and controls in addition to wing leading edges.

Name	Function	Floor area	Opened	Closed
Wilts And Dorset Bus Company, Castle Street	Wings	18,000 sq ft	16-10-40	31-10-45
Land Behind Rising Sun, Salisbury Street	---	15,000 sq ft	20-10-40	31-12-45
Wessex Garage, New Street	Fuselages, wing leading edges and tail units	15,000 sq ft	<30-10-40	31-12-45
Anna Valley Garage, Castle Street	Wing leading edges, tail units, sub-assemblies	13,720 sq ft	<30-11-40	30-11-45
Chattis Hill Aerodrome	Final assembly, flight test, storage when production ceased	31,350 sq ft	11-40	30-5-48
Witt and Vincent Garage, Devizes Road	Aluminium welding and manufacturing fuel tanks	Unknown	Unknown	Unknown
High Post Aerodrome	Final assembly, flight test	Unknown	27-2-41	31-5-47
	Experimental flight test	48,771 sq ft	6-6-43	2-47
High Post Hotel	High Post Hotel	Unknown	---	---
	Control tower (post June 1943)	Unknown	6/43	31-6-47
Assembly Rooms, Salisbury	Canteen	3,000 sq ft	10-7-41	31-5-46
Castle Street Garage, Chipper Lane	Transport	2,300 sq ft	10-7-41	31-5-46
Castle Road No. 1 Factory, Hudson's Field	Fuselage completion	16,148 sq ft	6-42	31-8-46
Castle Road	Canteen	2,800 sq ft	6-42	14-11-47
Castle Road No. 2 Factory	Leading edges, components	44,221 sq ft	5-43	14-11-47

Castle Road	Administration offices	Hutting	5-44	14-11-47
Castle Street, Nos. 18 & 21	Lock-up garages	Unknown	25-5-43	26-8-43

Total floor area: 210,310 sq ft
Number of aircraft produced that can be traced: 2,295

Trowbridge

Trowbridge's production line started up at the same time as those in Salisbury and Reading but lacked a suitable adjacent aerodrome. The Trowbridge units therefore fed into the Salisbury and Reading airfields until suitable take-off and landing facilities were found in 1943. The Forestreet Garage, Rutland Garage and Barnes Brothers in Southwick, were taken over before November 1940 and used for details, fittings, pipes and small components that fed into other production lines. In June 1941 in Westbury, the Laverton Cloth Mills was taken over as a raw materials and finished parts store and the Boulton Glove factory for assembly. Canteen facilities were found in The Red Triangle Club premises in 1942.

Meanwhile, work progressed on two new units in Trowbridge, by far the largest being in Bradley Road, built using salvageable structure from the Woolston works such as window frames. This was large enough to house an entire production line: fuselage and wing jigs were installed and sub-assemblies built with a tool room also established. All completed assemblies would be taken out to an RAF aerodrome opened in Keevil, where the Ministry of Aircraft Production had built on land requisitioned in 1941 a Type B1 hangar with airfield. The hangar is in use today as a farm building.

Completed items required storage and space was found wherever possible in local premises. For example, Curries Garage on Bath Road, Devizes, had an extension built to house completed fuselages. Aircraft in service also required effective support for spares that, in the case of the Spitfire, meant completed items such as a wing, undercarriage, propeller, even fuselages during a major repair. The last aeroplane, a Mk 24, flew out to No. 6 Maintenance Unit on 16 January 1947. Bradley Road finally closed in 1959.

Name	Function	Floor area	Opened	Closed
Fore Street Garage, Trowbridge	Details & fittings	9,300 sq ft	<30-11-40	30-6-45
Rutland Garage, Trowbridge	Pipes & coppersmiths	8,000 sq ft	<30-11-40	30-12-45
Barnes Brothers, Southwick Steam Roller Factory	Wing leading edges	16,916 sq ft	<30-11-40	28-2-46
Red Triangle Club	Canteen	4,216 sq ft	18-6-42	31-3-46
Laverton Cloth Mills, Westbury	Store, materials & finished parts	7,000 sq ft	29-6-41	31-10-46
Boulton Glove Company, Westbury	Bench assembly	Unknown	21-6-41	31-10-46
Hilperton Road Factory	Sub-assemblies	17,000 sq ft	1-42	30-4-46
Bradley Road Factory	Aircraft production line	85,770 sq ft	5-43	28-2-59
RAF Keevil Aerodrome	Final assembly, flight test	27,571 sq ft	7-43	30-1-48
Currie's Garage Bath Road, Devizes	Completed fuselage storage, extension behind the garage	Unknown	Unknown	Unknown
Moore's Garage, Bagshot	Transport dept	1,140 sq ft	6-4-42	12-1-46
Eyken's Garage, Kenilworth	Transport dept	2,500 sq ft	24-2-43	17-12-43

Total floor area: 179,413 sq ft
Number of aircraft produced that can be traced: 585

A WALK THROUGH SUPERMARINE'S HIDDEN DESIGN HQ

BY DAVID KEY

The future of the Spitfire had not one but two close calls in late 1940. Vital Spitfire plans escaped incineration when the office block at the Woolston plant that housed the design and accounts departments was struck during the bombing raid of 26 September. One projectile passed through the office and out the window, hitting the riverbank; another went straight through the floor but failed to explode. The plans and design team were moved during dispersal to the supposed safety of Southampton's University College but during the blitz on Southampton, one of the wooden huts that had been turned over to Supermarine was struck by incendiary bombs and burned down. Less than a week later, on 7 December 1940, Supermarine's design office began the process of clearing out of Southampton entirely and moving to the secluded grounds and stately isolation of Hursley Park in Hampshire.

Awaiting them was the recently widowed Lady Mary Cooper who, along with her late husband Sir George Cooper, had owned Hursley since 1902. Now alone in her Queen Anne-style house save for her servants and her son,

Supermarine's head office and top-secret design facilities relocated from Blitz-ravaged Southampton to the safety and seclusion of Hursley Park on the edge of the Hampshire Downs, where they expanded.

Lady Cooper welcomed Supermarine's management with flair, presenting them with a floral display in the shape of a Spitfire. Niceties over, the process of converting Hursley into a top-secret fighter plane design facility started. The Coopers had already removed most of their valuable property but there was no chance of moving the oak-panelled walls with richly gilded decorations, lined with massive Louis XV-style chinoiserie screens, so these had to be hidden behind particleboard.

Hursley's ground floor was turned over to Supermarine's design office, with the ballroom, drawing room, winter garden and the main corridor in the east wing all utilised for the new drawing office. Draughtsmen's tables were crammed into every available space. The technical office occupied the central hall and billiard room in the north-west corner, while the tracers moved into the morning – or Wedgwood – room. Joe Smith, head of Supermarine and chief designer since the passing of R.J. Mitchell, took over Sir George's office, while Supermarine's chief draughtsman, Eric Lovell-Cooper, took over Lady Cooper's boudoir.

Below, in the basement, the rooms were converted for the research department of chief metallurgist and head of research, Arthur Black, the laundry room was converted into a chemical store and laboratory, two of the servants' rooms were turned into a telephone exchange and the servants' dining hall became the staff canteen. Senior management used the Coopers' dining room on the ground floor as their own, executive 'mess'. Alongside the Supermarine staff, some of the

Designers and draughtsmen produced hand-drawn plans and documents vital to Spitfire construction.

Stella Rutter was poached from Portsmouth and the Royal Navy for her drawing skills to become part of a team of – ultimately – more than 150 at Hursley.

rooms retained their original use, including the butler's rooms linked to the massive strongroom, where the family silver was stored. In the kitchens, Lady Cooper's cook continued to provide meals alongside Supermarine canteen staff.

In the upper floors of the house the mix of Supermarine and household continued – for the short term. Lady Cooper occupied her suite of rooms on the first floor with her younger son. The old bedrooms and dressing rooms across the corridor, however, were now converted into offices for senior management and some of the accounts, subcontracts, purchasing and commercial departments.

Lady Cooper's servants were crammed into the attic rooms in the north-east corner of Hursley while a room in the south-east became the new drawing office for Supermarine's jig and tool design team. Works engineer Len Gooch and the planners, rate fixers and chasers occupied the remaining rooms on the attic floor.

One of the key changes enabled by the move to Hursley Park was the creation of a dedicated experimental department. The design team at Woolston had always been in close contact with the workforce, so could easily turn to them for modifications. This need for close co-operation had been highlighted during the development of the Spitfire in the 1930s. Then, Supermarine had been forced by the Air Ministry to subcontract much of the work, despite designs not having been finalised. Construction of wing and tail sub-assemblies was contracted out, while other companies would provide smaller components that often fell under the broad description of 'machined parts'. The process caused confusion and delays, which led to recriminations.

Mechanical test equipment was set up in the stables, while in the yard a Bellman hangar was erected to provide additional space for the structural test section under Oscar Sommer, one of the longest-serving members of Supermarine's technical office, and the new experimental department under department manager Frank Perry that was responsible for new prototype Spitfire marques. Another Bellman hangar was erected to the south of the stables to house the mill that processed wood used in mock-ups of new designs and some aircraft builds.

Supermarine took control of the entertainment hall, a long building between the stables and gardens, which was turned into a temporary, second drawing office until a design office in the form of a hangar capable of housing more than 150 draughtsmen was built. This hangar was partially buried in the ground and it was covered with camouflage netting in an attempt to avoid detection by enemy reconnaissance. A hut was erected to the north of the walled garden to house twenty draughtsmen from the jig and tool design office.

Moving the drawing office out of the house resulted in a major reorganisation. In order to maintain the close connection between the drawing office in the new hangar and the technical office and senior management in the house, the large windows in the conservatory facing the path to the drawing office were converted into doors. Space on either side of a new passageway was allocated to the tracers, making good use of natural light, while in the ballroom, a corridor was formed creating a large office space in the northern section of the room at the same time. This space, along with the drawing room, became the planning department, which ensured the correct design sheets were issued to the dispersal workshops and the Spitfire plant in Castle Bromwich.

The growth of the workforce began to put additional pressure on space and strain the relationship between Supermarine and Lady Cooper, although frustration had set in quite early on. Lady Cooper's youngest son, Alistair, engaged in some enthusiastic social drinking with the fire watch, while Lady Cooper was increasingly frustrated by groups of Supermarine staff loitering on the staircase and blocking her way when she tried to use it. At the same time, according to his daughter Barbara Harries, Supermarine head Joe Smith is said to have been annoyed at interruptions to his meetings in what had been Sir George Cooper's office when Lady Cooper's butler would pop in to remove ready cash from the safe. It was time for Lady Cooper to leave. The most common story as to how and why this happened was that a fire was deliberately started by one of her household staff in June 1942, highlighting the problems of having unvetted domestic staff in a supposedly secure location. Lady Cooper was forced to find alternative accommodation and moved out at the end of 1942, never to return.

The departure of Lady Cooper meant Supermarine was able to further expand and reorganise. Her large master bedroom, in the middle of the first floor overlooking the south lawn, became the boardroom with all main departments attending weekly production meetings. Alistair Cooper's rooms in the south-west corner of the first floor and Lady Cooper's dressing rooms became offices for senior management, including Len Gooch. On the attic floor, the suite of rooms used by Lady Cooper's servants was converted into the office for the subcontract department under Denis Le Penn Webb.

Expansion in the grounds was moving apace, too. With the relocation of the drawing office into its new hangar to the east of the house, the entertainment hall next to the stables was converted into a mould loft where draughtsmen's designs were turned into full-size versions as pattern pieces.

Additional huts were erected on the route from the mansion house to the drawing office. Immediately next to the east wing was the drawing library: in the initial stages of the move to Hursley, the design drawing archive had been stored in a farm building at Sleepy Hollow in nearby Ampfield. Further along the path to the drawing office, alongside the northern wall of the kitchen garden, a hut was put in place for the jig and tool drawing office, moving them out of their first-floor rooms in the house. To cope with the increased number of staff, a new canteen was also built next to the new drawing office hangar. By 1945, the drawing office had been further extended with the addition of four smaller huts alongside the main hangar building.

Apart from the new drawing office, the most significant change was for the experimental department, who subsequently moved out of the stable yard into a new, much larger, hangar close to the Southampton Lodge entrance to the estate. When they moved, they had to manually lift a partially completed fuselage, navigate it through the archway at the entrance to the stables and then carry it the mile around the estate road to the new hangar. The experimental hangar, completed in the fourth quarter of 1944, provided the space to make complete prototype aircraft. These would be assembled, engines attached and run to test them in the plane before being disassembled, loaded onto Queen Mary trailers and transported to Worthy Down and later High Post for reassembly and flight testing. The proximity of the experimental hangar to the village school meant that, when the engines were tested, the noise was such that classes had to be suspended.

The expansion of the various offices and departments reflected the growing number of staff, needed to meet the ever greater demands on Supermarine for variants of the Spitfire. New designs such as the Spiteful, planned successor to the Spitfire, began in 1943. Expansion also reflected a rationalisation of the

Supermarine organisation, with some of the departments initially dispersed to isolated locations being brought back together with the main headquarters staff at Hursley. As part of the rationalisation, a substantial part of the Aeronautical Inspection Directorate (AID), who inspected engines and airframes at every stage and who had been moved to Holt House in Bassett immediately following the raids on Southampton, were moved to Hursley.

Hursley had come a long way in a short time: from a secluded stately home to crucible of the Spitfire.

HOW TO HIDE A WORKFORCE

BY DAVID KEY

Supermarine had successfully hidden its design department at Hursley House, but the location presented a fresh problem: how to get the skilled designers, draughtsmen and engineers critical to the design and testing of the Spitfire to their new offices. For the majority of the workforce still living in Southampton 10 miles (16km) away, one answer came in the shape of a fleet of double-decker buses that ran to and from Hursley every day.

Gordon Monger, living in the village at that time and who would later work on experimental Spitfires at Worthy Down and then at Hursley itself, recalls being woken by his grandfather one morning to witness the buses arriving in Hursley, swaying precariously as they navigated the country lanes. Indeed, the drivers are reported to

Gordon Monger witnessed double-decker buses loaded with Supermarine's designers, draughtsmen and engineers destined for Hursley.

have raced down these lanes at breakneck speeds, their feats immortalised in a cartoon in Supermarine's unofficial in-house magazine, *Ragazine*. For some, these commutes could be a social highlight, perhaps meeting future partners for the first time on the journeys, while for others they were merely an uncomfortable and chilly experience.

For security reasons none of the buses carried any indication of their destination and staff had to work out which bus to take, based on whether they could see colleagues on board. Hursley was supposed to be a covert operation but it was impossible to keep the purpose of the buses completely secret. Harry Griffiths, assistant to Arthur Black who was head of Supermarine's Research Department, tells us: 'I was on a service bus going from Southampton to Winchester when we met three of the staff buses on the way home and I heard a lady sitting behind me say to her friend: "That's all the Spitfire people going home from Hursley." Thankfully the enemy was not listening.'

A fleet of double-decker buses outside the house could also have been picked up on aerial reconnaissance by the Luftwaffe, with potentially disastrous consequences. Denis Le Penn Webb, as Supermarine's transport manager, was tasked with finding a way to hide the buses during the day. His solution was to use some of the rubble from the bombed Woolston works to construct a hardstanding for them under the trees by the Winchester Lodge entrance to Hursley. The trees would fulfil the same protective role for Allied soldiers based at Hursley during the build-up to D-Day a few years later.

The buses provided the vital link for a large proportion of the workforce but for others who'd lost their homes to Luftwaffe bombs in Southampton, it was a case of seeking lodgings closer to Hursley. Some accommodation could be found by billeting with local residents but empty rooms were in short supply in Hursley and the surrounding villages. Some families were fortunate enough to land local cottages to rent while others found themselves crammed into just one room. For many of these families the move was not simply a change in the size of their homes, it was also a step back in time as many properties lacked mod cons. People were forced to draw water from wells in the absence of a mains supply, while even at Hursley House there was a lack of flush toilets and some waste had to be removed nightly.

Accommodation was possibly one of the biggest hindrances to the completion of the dispersal. In the Vickers-Armstrongs Quarterly Report for Supermarine in the first quarter of 1941, it was recounted that great difficulty had been encountered in transferring skilled men from Southampton 'because of the impossibility of getting sufficient and suitable housing'.

One answer was to erect prefabricated housing close by – an approach employed in several dispersal areas. A group of approximately eighty temporary, prefabricated, single-storey houses called The Hutments was built, less than a mile from Hursley on the route taken by the works buses from Chandler's Ford. Each unit was built in a semi-detached style to house two families and was intended as a short-term solution, although they were still in use, albeit with some modifications, after Supermarine's departure from Hursley in the late 1950s. For the family of draughtsman Oswald Bell, who'd been crammed into a single cottage room, The Hutments were a welcome escape, if a little basic. 'They were very damp and cold, but I guess we just got on with it,' daughter Eileen recalls. 'We were desperate because we were homeless. My father wanted the end one because it had quite a large garden.'

THIS ISLAND SALISBURY: WAR COMES TO THE CITY

Although war had been declared in September 1939, it wasn't until months later that those on the home front in towns and cities such as Salisbury got their first taste of the conflict to come, beyond the worry of evacuation and what had been the tedious realities of blackouts and rationing. It was in May 1940, just months ahead of the Southampton bombings and Supermarine setting up in Salisbury, that hundreds of thousands of exhausted British, French and Belgian troops began arriving by boat from Dunkirk. The residents of Salisbury were about to discover that the Phoney War – the period between the declaration of war and the start of the German onslaught in the West – really was over.

Ray Elliott, 10 when the war started, explains that wake-up:

My cousin and I came home from swimming one day and sat inside our house were two of the scruffiest soldiers I'd ever seen: they were unshaven, unwashed, dishevelled, their uniforms were dirty and torn. Mum told us: 'I found them in the road and they looked a bit dazed, so I brought them in for a cup of tea.' They didn't seem to know how they got into this state, where they came from or what they were going to do.

These were chaotic and confused days and the returning troops lacked direction. Ray's dad took the pair to the cinema but en route they ran into friends in Salisbury's market square and went on their way – never to be seen again. Ray continues:

A few days later we realised what had happened. They'd just been brought back from the beaches of Dunkirk – brought back in the boats, dumped at Southampton, put on a train and sent to Salisbury. They had been told to get off with no guidance or anything. The main thing was they'd been rescued, I suppose, but the war had become a reality for me.

With Dunkirk came fear of invasion and so it was in those early days that Salisbury and the surrounding areas were hastily prepared to meet the expected enemy influx. The German game plan was clear: their commanders would repeat their plan for air attack and rapid land advances should they successfully manage to cross the Channel, bringing Blitzkrieg to the British mainland. Having abandoned large amounts of weapons and equipment in the evacuation from Dunkirk, the British military command decided the best tactic was to delay any advance. This meant

Left: Tank traps were part of a system of natural and man-made defences called GHQ Lines intended to slow down any invasion force should it arrive. Right: Viewed from above, such traps were difficult to spot but can be seen here highlighted.

establishing fifty defensive lines known as General Headquarters (GHQ) Lines that divided the country into sections with the aim of slowing down the enemy and protecting vital areas. At least four of these lines would run in relatively close proximity to the new locations of the Supermarine factories.

The GHQ Lines combined natural features, such as rivers and valleys, with man-made defences. Anti-tank ditches and concrete or brick pillboxes were hastily erected during a building frenzy in 1940 that would also see some 50,000 anti-tank mines laid by June. Narrow gaps in these defensive lines served as crossing points and would fall under the watchful eye of defenders if and when the time came. GHQ Green Line was the outer defence of Bristol and its great docks and ran north–south to protect against attack from the east, but it came within 35 miles (56.3km) of what were to become the Spitfire factories of Salisbury and 5.7 miles (9.1km) of those in Trowbridge. The Reading factories were close to two GHQ Lines: just a few miles separated Spitfire production from GHQ Red Line, which ran from Malmesbury in Wiltshire to Tilehurst in Berkshire and GHQ Blue Line, which started at the Kennet and Avon Canal in the South-West. A completely man-made line, meanwhile, ran from the GHQ Green Line at Freshford to Odiham in Hampshire via Salisbury.

Sited at the confluence of five rivers, Salisbury was considered a naturally defensible position. One of these rivers – the Avon – formed part of a north–south stop line that ran from Salisbury to Ringwood, again to hinder the enemy's east–west movement. This line featured three river crossings complete with pillboxes. Defences in and around the city were also reinforced with the addition of pillboxes hidden in ingenious locations, including behind stone walls on farms along Wilton Road to the north-west of Salisbury, skirting the River Nadder. Existing features such as bridges were equipped with new firing positions. One, the Laverstock Road Bridge, even had its walls filled with flammable liquid that could be ignited when the enemy came close enough. On top of this, inevitably, came barrage balloons floating above Salisbury, designed to force enemy aircraft into higher attack positions where they couldn't be as accurate and where they would become susceptible to defensive ground fire.

Of course, there was the blackout, too: all domestic, workplace and public lights were covered at night to deny enemy aircraft the means of identifying targets on the ground. 'One thing I remember principally about the war was the blackout,' says Stan Gordon, welding at Witt and Vincent Garage. 'You can't imagine life without any lights! Just a glimmer here and there.'

Salisbury telegram boy Gordon Topp was expected to deliver messages up until 7 p.m., meaning that during the short days of winter when the sun set early, the job of finding addresses and house numbers became all the more difficult:

Every house had to make sure there was no light showing and the air raid wardens, if they saw a little gap in the windows, they'd shout out: 'Put that light out!' Even a little crack. They used to kid everybody that German aircraft could see somebody with a cigarette lit down below. Salisbury was in complete darkness – just like you were in a country village with no lights on whatsoever and it was quite difficult cycling around.

As the fear of invasion subsided, there came fresh reason to keep the city secure as Spitfire production picked up at the newly formed secret sites. Gordon recalls being surprised by the level of protection afforded to a place that outwardly seemed to offer little strategic value:

I was always amazed at the amount of protection the city had – all the anti-tank ditches built around the town and then there's five rivers through the centre, which were a protection. Where there wasn't any protection from the rivers, tank traps were built and ditches dug – so that tanks couldn't get through. We had barrage balloons all the way around Salisbury – most of the schools had a barrage balloon, and they were winched up every time the air raid siren went.

Bill Edwards, who came to work on Spitfires at Castle Road, concurs as he'd noticed a high degree of security in and around Salisbury in the days before he started work:

I couldn't really understand why they had all the barrage balloons up, day in and day out, and that the army was stationed there with their guns. It looked as if they were well prepared for any trouble, but it never came.

As the build-up to Operation Overlord and the D-Day landings began, so the military presence around the Spitfire factories changed from one of defence to one that was preparing to take the fight to the enemy across the Channel. Invasion was coming, but not of Britain. Rather, it would be on the beaches of Normandy in north-west France. D-Day was to be the start of the liberation of Europe and would become the largest combined military operation in history, with 150,000 troops landed in just one day – 6 June 1944.

Salisbury became a major centre of preparation. US General Dwight D. Eisenhower, Supreme Commander of Allied forces in Europe, and Britain's Field Marshal Bernard Montgomery, who was to command ground forces in Normandy for D-Day, met in the grounds of Eisenhower's headquarters at Wilton House to the north-west of the city. Wilton House had been requisitioned by the Army in 1940 to become headquarters of the Southern Command, an area that ran from Sussex in the South-East to the tip of Cornwall in the South-West. The stately home's

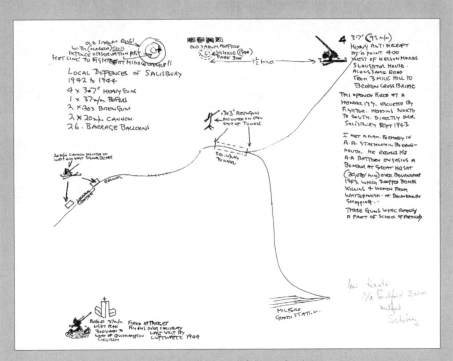

Local milk delivery boy Ken Hayter sketched the defences of Salisbury.

Salisbury, like other towns that housed Supermarine's factories, was not completely immune from air attack.

Salisbury became a major centre for US troop deployments and planning ahead of D-Day in June 1944.

communications had been upgraded to cope with the installation of 750 miles of telephone cable to link this command centre to surrounding units. Wilton House's facilities were expanded with the addition of extra offices and accommodation using Nissen huts, while the estate office was converted into a canteen and the nearby Pembroke Arms Hotel turned over to an officers' mess.[7] It was in Wilton House's sumptuous Double Cube Room that the cream of the Allied military and political command would convene to plan and strategise D-Day – not just Eisenhower and Montgomery but British Prime Minister Winston Churchill, leader of the Free French, General Charles de Gaulle, and other senior military figures.

The militarisation of Salisbury continued outside the walls of this elite hub. Breamore House, near Fordingbridge, served as headquarters for the American 7th Corps and the 3rd Army, while all units converged on Salisbury Plain to conduct military exercises. On the eve of D-Day, troops landing by sea left Salisbury for embarkation at Poole, Portland and Weymouth in Dorset.

As a child, Doreen Andrews lived near the Spitfire factory at the premises of the Wilts and Dorset Bus Garage on Castle Street. She remembers streams of tanks whose metal tracks would rip up the road's surface and armed guards who kept watch on the city. For all that, the presence was far from threatening:

The US troops had lorries parked up on Castle Street by the coach station and there was a sentry box with a solider always standing in it on duty. Well, my mum became friendly with two of the lads who'd be on duty and they used to come to the house.

Doreen recounts, too, a tale from the local lad she would eventually marry:

The Americans were also parked in their lorries up on the top of Devizes Road and they were given the order to go, that must have been D-Day. My husband later told me how they'd thrown all their chewing gum away and that he'd col-lected the wrappers – I've still got them upstairs. And packs of cards! And he went up with his friends and collected all of these things.

Joan Johns, who tested the piston rings that went into the Spitfire's powerful Rolls-Royce engines at Wellworthy, vividly recalls the scale of the military build-up, with local roads choked by tanks and trucks in their green camouflage paint. 'I cycled everywhere,' Joan recalls enthusiastically. 'I used to cycle out to a farm at Winterbourne a few miles outside Salisbury and before D-Day the roads were lined with army vehicles. They were all preparing to go down to the coast.'

Not all troops who fought in Normandy landed by sea – some 23,000 were flown in. They were US and British airborne soldiers who jumped from transport planes such as the US-made Douglas C-47s, or descended on the fields of Normandy in British-manufactured, wooden Horsa gliders that would be towed by powered aircraft. These airborne troops went in ahead of the seaborne landings to prepare the ground, seize control of vital structures such as bridges, and take out enemy positions from behind as they fired on beaches to prevent Allied troops coming ashore.

Living at home with her mum and brothers back in Salisbury was Adele Stokes. She got to witness the mighty Allied armada as it departed:

It was quite an exciting time, but the time that really upset everybody – my mother in particular – was when we heard all the planes going over for the end of the war. It was thousands and thousands in the sky. My mother said: 'Oh my word, this is it,' and we didn't know what she meant, because we were little. But you looked at the bombers going over ... and you were sad and tearful, because you knew so many were not going to come back.

DAY IN THE LIFE
OF A FACTORY

If anybody captured the popular image of women working in Britain's wartime factories, it was Ruby Loftus. Ruby was immortalised in a 1943 Ministry of Information poster in blue dungarees, red scarf and green hair net, carefully leaning into a lathe working on a breach ring. This breach ring was considered a vital component for a Bofors anti-aircraft (AA) gun and making such a part demanded the utmost skill and attention. The purpose of this poster was clear: it was commissioned by the Government to boost recruitment of women in industry. Ruby was no artist's fiction as you might expect; she was a real person performing a real role. Ruby did indeed make breach rings and she did so at the massive Royal Ordnance Factory No. 11, a facility of up to 2,000 workers on Newport's Corporation Road turning out guns such as the Bofors.

The Spitfire was no mere AA gun. Indeed, the women of the secret Spitfire factories were taking on a task that some considered near impossible: building an all-metal aircraft whose sculpted curves and smooth finish required construction and engineering techniques that did not easily lend themselves to the kinds of rapid, large-scale output required of wartime.

Chris Michelle, workshop manager with modern-day restoration and manufacturing specialist Airframe Assemblies on the Isle of Wight, puts the task these workers faced into perspective against the construction techniques used for the Spitfire's chief Battle of Britain adversary, the German Messerschmitt Bf 109. Both aircraft were of monocoque construction, using metal skin and airframe to bear the ripping stresses and strains of flight and fight. 'Consider the simplicity of the way the Germans went about things,' Chris tells us. 'The fuselage frames are integrated with the skin, all pressed in one great piece. So you have a series of these special, formed-up panels to make the back of the airplane, from the back of the cockpit to the place where the fin bolts on, in thirty pieces, whereas in the Spitfire it's more like 300 pieces,' he says. 'The Spitfire had its advantages, in that it could be built in small factories and small units, and repaired in the field. The Me 109 was lovely and simple to build, but you needed some serious factory kit to knock them out and that meant they didn't lend themselves to small-scale production.'

Pundits may have been right about the theoretical difficulties but their conclusions were proved wrong. What they hadn't counted on was the ingenuity of Supermarine in addressing the engineering and manufacturing challenge – or on the patriotism, pride and energy of its workforce. Supermarine's 'Rubys', plucked from the 9–5 of retail or rarefied worlds of service, would find the realities of long shifts and heavy work a stark contrast. But they adapted and thrived.

Pat Pearce entered the Supermarine system at the Wilts and Dorset Bus Company in Salisbury, building wings. She had chosen factory work over the Women's Land Army, where she would have contributed to the nation's food and agricultural supply by working with crops and animals, tending reclaimed land or serving in forestry. Fresh from the relative serenity of Marks & Spencer, she describes the cacophony of that first morning – a din of drilling, hammering, music on the radio and machines that seemed to never get turned off. 'The noise was the first thing that hit you,' Pat exclaims. 'It was frightening really ... there were all these people just ready to start on their jobs and we were right over the other side. It got so noisy you could hardly even hear yourself speak.'

Work was around the clock, divided into day and night shifts, from 8 a.m. to 7 p.m. and from 8 p.m. to 7 a.m., with workers performing a month on nights followed by a month on days and so on. With the nation on a wartime footing, factories operated 365 days a year to meet demand for Spitfires, with the added incentive of bonuses to try and help increase output. Pat became a fitter's assistant and found the pace blistering. 'We used to chat to one another, but not hang about because the men you worked with were a bit on the "spritz" side – they were all for getting the bonus! It was very busy all the time. You didn't hang about – nobody did. They were very busy workers. They all had a job,' Pat tells us.

Spitfire production was essential to the war effort and Supermarine was busy trying to hit delivery targets. After the late delivery of those first Spitfire orders, nothing could be allowed to slow things down once Supermarine had reorganised, hired the necessary staff and established a working system. Management therefore kept a close eye on the shop floor to make sure everybody was busy and took a dim view of any workers who appeared to be slowing down by taking an unscheduled break or causing a distraction for others. Former hairdresser Bette Blackwell was assigned to Wessex Motors in Salisbury, a site dedicated to the building of Spitfire fuselages, tail units and the leading edges of those trademark wings that Pat helped build. Bette explains just how meticulously Supermarine watched the shop floor:

They seemed to time us in everything we did. If they saw you leave your job and go out to the ladies' cloakroom that was all right, but if you left your job and walked to another part of the factory because you were going to talk to somebody that was wrong – they didn't like you talking. One day they had us all together and they said: 'You are in here to work, not to talk, to work.'

Talking wasn't the only activity discouraged, as management paid close attention for signs of fraternisation and potential distraction:

I had these American dimes and I wanted to get the holes drilled in them using the benches in the Spitfire factory. There were men working with these small drills so I mentioned this to one of them, thinking he might make the holes for me, and he said to come over when nobody is looking. So I took my dimes one day to do it and his chargehand came over and said: 'What do you think you're doing!'

The Wilts and Dorset bus garage where Pat worked was an 18,000 sq ft (1,672 sq m) facility partitioned by a wall across the middle, meaning Spitfire production could proceed in one part while being hidden by the everyday activities of the bus garage in the other. With little time to chat and the pace non-stop, it was quite possible to get cut off from your fellow workers, even in such a reduced workspace. 'A cousin of mine was working there – he lived in Salisbury,' Pat says. 'I saw him years ago and I said: "Remember when we worked in the [Spitfire] factory?" and he said: "You weren't there, were you?" And I said I was and he said: "That's the first I've heard of it!"

Joan Little was at Hilperton Road, Trowbridge, also working on wings. Having transferred from domestic service, she recounts that first morning's shock of the new with her fellow recruits, waiting to be told where to start and what to do. 'As soon as you got in there, the manager was rushing around to sort everyone out and we were standing there like lemons – we were left out there waiting and wondering. We were eager to get going, but he was too busy with other people,' she says.

Joyce Hunt, also at Hilperton Road, explains what happened next. 'When we got there, they got us together in bunches and told us the work they would like us to do. We started off with small things for a Spitfire and gradually worked our way up. And my partner and I – Phyllis – we had a set of girls that did Spitfire rings.'

Night shifts could be a little more forgiving, according to Pat. 'On day shift you felt you were being watched all the time, but the foreman didn't go on nights – there was this little chargehand. If you felt like a little sleep, you could go and have a lie down!'

'The happiest time of my life' – the verdict of Joan Little, here (right) with sister Betty Potter, on her time at Supermarine's Trowbridge factory.

Joyce Kolk, first left, in the official issue dungarees that Supermarine gave its new intake of women workers.

Joyce agrees – she also preferred working on the assembly line at night. 'You had more room and you could do more work,' she says.

At other factories, workers favoured day shifts because it was thought safer, as it was mostly at night when German bombers would strike factories and cities. Supermarine had gone to great lengths to prepare the factory facilities for the new recruits, with the careful installation of jigs and other equipment vital to the manufacturing process. One thing they overlooked, however, was the fact that women would make up so much of this new workforce. Before the war, factory shop floors had been all-male bastions and Supermarine had done little to cater to the changing times – at least in terms of the uniform the women employees were expected to wear. Dungarees were the norm and while fine for the boys and men of Supermarine's workforce, they were badly fitting for the women who made up the majority of its workers. Bette would be one of thousands who'd cut and customise their dungarees. She recalls:

Factories such as Bradley Road, Trowbridge, were a baptism of fire for those coming from a life of working in retail or domestic service.

Joyce Hunt (centre): 'Everybody was so friendly, there was always a joke going along. You were working for the same thing, being a war on.'

They gave me these dungarees and I said: 'I'm not wearing those.' And they said: 'But you've got to.' So I went out into the cloakroom and I put these dungarees on and the crotch came down to my knees! And I had to roll them up and up and up, bottoms and all, and they kept falling down. And I kept falling over myself. So I took them home and cut them off. The crotch was still too low mind, but they were a bit more comfortable.

Supermarine was better prepared to meet the needs of its new intake in areas more directly related to the work. A nucleus of specialised tradesmen who'd worked in the Southampton plants had moved up to serve in the local factories but the bulk of the fresh recruits required training in the fundamentals of metalwork required to build the Spitfire. Many received in-house training from foremen marching up and down to keep an eye on performance and quality. Others went out-of-house for more specialised training in tasks such as welding, and would go on to become skilled workers. Among them, Stan Gordon at the Witt and Vincent Garage – a unit that specialised in welding and in production of tanks for Spitfires.

Stan, along with three other 16-year-old lads, was sent to industrial giant British Oxygen, where they were inducted into the ways of welding. This required a light touch and a high standard of workmanship to meet the demanding requirements of aviation in general but even more so for the Spitfire. Stan describes the set-up at Witt and Vincent once he'd been trained: 'Us welders were in a line, half were women and there were my three mates. The women were doing exactly the same as the men – there was no distinction at all. We were all in this together.'

Stan Gordon at Witt and Vincent received specialised training in welding to work on the all-metal Spitfire. 'The women were doing exactly the same as the men – there was no distinction at all.'

Riveting was also fundamental to the Spitfire, thanks to the plane's innovative, all-metal frame that used an early form of hardened aluminium called duraluminium. Other RAF aircraft of the time still employed combinations of metal, wood and fabric that required bolts and stitching in addition to metal fixing. But for the Spitfire, it was welding and riveting all the way.

Riveting was a skilled trade and riveters were brought up from Southampton to help get the ball rolling, but gradually more people were being trained, with the women doing much of the work. 'If you showed them what to do and what not to do, they could go at it ad infinitum. Each application could be different, but riveting is riveting is riveting,' says Spitfire historian and former Vickers Supermarine engineer Norman Parker. The Spitfire employed two types of riveting. One involved a toggle gun, a device with a U-shaped attachment that fitted around a surface to close up the rivet. The second was reaction riveting, a two-person job: one would hammer the rivet through a hole with a rivet gun while a second person – called a 'holder-upper' – would press a block against the other side to catch the rivet as the tail came through.

Bette was one of those inducted into riveting – undertaking both types. She was handed a toggle gun by the chargehand on her first day and introduced to riveting on the assembly line:

> You had to bend down all the time to use it. You put the bottom part on the underside and you put the rivet in the top, and you'd go all the way along and press the lever and it would knock the rivets down. It was damned heavy, and you had to get into such awkward corners with them. You'd have to aim the gun up in the air, although I did have my shoulder to lean on when I did it that way.
>
> So then they put me on 'holding up' and that was holding up rivets for somebody else with a rivet gun – the noise was terrific. I happened to be with this man who was the son of the factory boss and I would have to wait for him to do something because you couldn't hear each other shouting to communicate. It was so loud! The noise was going 'Brrr, brrr, brrr' all day long. I had to be in the aircraft body while he was on the outside riveting. I think they gave me that job because I was small and could easily get inside – I'd screw myself up into a little ball.

The equipment may have been heavy and conditions cramped, but standards were exacting and precision was everything – the Spitfire was a design-led piece of fine engineering and each step in the build process interlinked. Spitfire sub-assemblies were made per plane and there were no surplus piles – for example, wings were made in pairs for each fuselage. This meant any slip-ups or mistakes in that production line could throw out the whole process and introduce delay. 'I had a girl who was my holder-upper. She got told off once, too, because she made me go nearly through the plate of the aircraft,' Bette remembers.

The process was regimented. 'You knew what you were doing and you knew what you had to do. You'd been trained up. A lot of the girls ... would be shown what was required, how it was to be done and basically they'd get on and do it. It would be repetitive in that sense,' Norman says.

You were assigned to one specific task in the overall assembly puzzle: illustrating this was Joyce Kolk, who worked on wings at the Wilts and Dorset in Salisbury before moving to the Wessex Garage, also in Salisbury, where her focus was the wheel housings. It might have been regimented and physically uncomfortable but it was liberating for the new intake. 'I used to love riveting,' admits Joan, who made handheld rings – up to sixty per shift – at the Hilperton Road factory. 'We had a foreman who used to walk up and down and tell us what to do for twelve hours every night. There was no chance of sitting down – that's why we developed varicose veins!' Joan says.

They built the Spitfire in three main sections – fuselage, wings and tail that, in turn, were made of a number of sub-assemblies. Each factory had been assigned one or a number of sections to build, or they worked on building important sub-components such as wing leading edges at Wessex Motors, or fuel tanks. Making the Spitfire in sections demanded the use of huge frames, called jigs – strong, rigid structures with location points for holding fuselage frames, wing ribs, tail pieces and other sections firmly in position for construction – before they were moved to the next stage on another jig in another part of the factory. Supermarine's jig and tool teams had worked to close and careful limits during installation. Attachment points could be adjusted to meet required dimensions, ensuring precision in construction and allowing the tools to interoperate and be interchanged.

The foundation of the fuselage was made up of nineteen duraluminium frames that formed a skeleton and were responsible for the Spitfire's curved and tapering shape. These frames ran from just behind the propeller all the way to the tail-fin at the rear of the aeroplane, reducing in size to help aerodynamics. Air tanks, cable runs and load-bearing supports would run down the inside of this structure.

Three sub-assemblies went into making one fuselage section: one for the engine (that would be installed later); a main unit that included the cockpit; and the tail-fin section at the rear. The cockpit was a sub-assembly built on its own jig before being combined with the engine section and another section that ran from behind the cockpit to the tail-fin on a larger, different jig. Pick-ups to hold the engine and wings were bolted on before everything was moved to a main fuselage jig where the alloy skin would be applied. The skin was made from

The High Post Aerodrome Hotel before Supermarine took over.

The very modern Amesbury All Electric Petrol Station was a local landmark serving pre-war drivers and bike riders on the A345, Salisbury–Amesbury Road.

High Post Aerodrome became one of the few centres for experimentation.

duraluminium that arrived in large sheets. These were cut to form plates of varying thickness, measured using a system known as Standard Wire Gauge and with imperial and metric equivalents – 24 (0.22in/0.558cm), 20 (0.036in/0.914cm) and 18 gauge (0.48in 1.219cm) – reducing in thickness towards the tail and fixed in place using rivets. The fuselage was now moved to another jig for the addition of holes to take wings, before everything was cleaned and sent for painting in the RAF's green and brown camouflage.

Moving this fuselage was a challenge. The Spitfire had been designed by Mitchell with wheels on the wings, and the wings weren't added until later at airfield factories down the line – places such as Chattis Hill and High Post. Factory workers therefore relied on a set of special, wheeled trestles that would fit into the airframe just in front of the unfinished cockpit. While the main fuselage came together, workers built the tail unit. This comprised four frames, eight tail formers and load-bearing supports, and was covered in a 22-gauge (0.28in/0.711cm) alloy skin. The tail-fin unit, a relatively simple job consisting of two spars and covered in 24-gauge alloy, was joined to a tail-fin piece before the completed unit was joined to the main fuselage.

Bill Edwards was an eyewitness to the work of painting the Spitfires. Bill had landed work at the Castle Road factories in Old Sarum thanks to his aunt who worked there. Initially helping out generally, Bill became more specialised with experience, working with wiring looms and installing engines in the fuselages at Castle Road factory No. 1. One of Bill's early jobs involved assisting an electrician, scrambling about to help fit a switch unit that had to be introduced to the Spitfire to remind pilots to retract the undercarriage after take-off. Pilots converting to the Spitfire from older RAF fighters meant they came from biplanes whose undercarriage remained down, in a fixed position. 'The work I did was to help everybody because, though I was of general use ... Mitch, who was one of the electricians, would come to me and say: "Bill, I've got that blooming switch to put in that tailplane again!"'

Bill Edwards remembers the fumes in the Spitfire paint shop on Castle Road. 'I don't know how some of those girls got through the day.'

Painting of body sub-assemblies took place at factory No. 2, where women worked with chemical-based paints and little protection. The shocking conditions made a lasting impression on Bill:

I remember going down there one day and, oh, the fumes. I don't know how some of those girls got through the day. It was really bad, I felt sorry for them. There was a sort of screen around it, but when you start spraying in a factory like that there was no way to keep it in and I don't think they were wearing any masks either.

Nothing illustrated the challenge of building the Spitfire better than those instantly recognisable elliptical wings. Building these unique structures was the most complex part of the construction and involved a series of steps. Each wing comprised two separately built sections – the leading edge and main wing. One of the roles of the Wessex Garage where Bette was stationed in Salisbury was to produce wing leading edges that would then be used in the main wing assembled by Pat and her workmates at the Wilts and Dorset. Other factories, such as Castle Road No. 2 in Salisbury, would produce both the leading edge and the full wing.

The leading edge was like a knife used to slice the air that ran over the wing and would have to endure tremendous pressure. It was built around a metal, D-shaped torsion box – a unit comprising a series of internal chambers that had the advantage of providing great strength while being light. This structure would be cut and joined together, with the main wing section built using a series of metal spars that ran the span of the wing with girder-like booms across.

Flanges that would allow the alloy skin to be attached to the leading edge were riveted into place along the front faces of the booms, while a single sheet of 14-gauge (0.80in/2.03cm) duraluminium was pressed to form the skin and riveted into place on the spar booms. Holes for gun ports were cut into the skin, along with holes that would allow factory workers to reach inside for the fit-out phase of construction – the addition of internal elements such as wiring and the ordnance. Pat recalls the constant flow of pre-cut alloy plates arriving at the bus garage:

> Big metal plates would come in and they'd fix them on to the framework every day and he [the fitter] marked them out where we had to drill. Then he put the plates on and cut all around. The same thing happened every day with two of us doing something different to the wing.

The need to work the metal applied to other parts, too. Stan recalls shaping metal at Witt and Vincent. 'I can remember having sheets of aluminium that I had to put oil on and heat up to make them soft, before hammering them into shape with wooden mallets and welding the seam.'

Once the wing sections were complete, they were brought together on a third jig. The leading edge was set in a downward-facing position, trailing edge ribs riveted to the rear spar, bays added for the engine radiator and for the wheels of the retractable undercarriage, and the skin attached using countersunk rivets. It was painstaking and precise work – but rewarding. Joyce says:

> When you put the nuts and bolts in that held them onto the big booms, you had to be very, very careful not to scrape the paint off. I enjoyed it, because it was more like man's work. It was really interesting to make the ribs and put them on the booms. We all put our heart and soul into it, because we all wanted the Spitfires. We were told one year by a pilot: 'Whatever you do, we have got very few Spitfires, please keep the work up and do your best to make the Spitfires.' That's what we did.

If you weren't working on jigs you were manning workbenches, two people to a bench, row upon row. On the work went. Royal visits were a staple routine for

Castle Road Factory No. 2, in the tranquil setting of Old Sarum, was built especially to handle wing construction and wing leading edges.

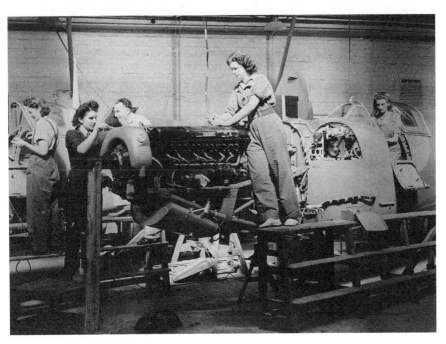

Teams huddled in small groups around Spitfires working on designated functions, here at Castle Road Factory No. 2.

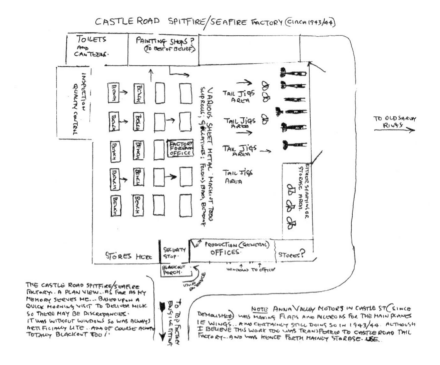

Inside Castle Road Factory No. 1, as depicted by milk delivery boy Ken Hayter.

wartime factories to help boost morale and Trowbridge was no exception. Local boy Stanley Jones remembers how word would escape, despite the visits being made – or at least announced – at short notice, as when Queen Mary, the widow of King George V, took a tour of Spitfire wing assembly on one of her frequent trips to Trowbridge:

> We heard from a lady working at one of the Spitfire factories that the Queen was coming. I always recall this being on a Saturday afternoon and accordingly just a group of us children waited on the corner of Victoria Road, which was on the outskirts of the town. Sure enough, the royal car drew up and out stepped Queen Mary, prim as always with rolled umbrella, and she went into the factory. Just us, a small group of officials and Her Majesty![18]

The short-notice nature of the tours gave management and workers inside little time to clean up and make ready. For her part, Joyce refused to obey the clean-up order. 'Our boss said: 'Everybody's got to wear clean overalls,' and I said to my mate: 'I can't see this, she's coming to see us work. Why have we got to clean up our benches and wear clean overalls? She's coming to see people working here.' And whose bench did she stop at? Ours! He weren't very happy,' Joyce says with a laugh.

The Spitfire's internals were now fitted before the metal was cleaned and painted. Those internals included conduits for cables that let the pilot control ailerons, elevators and rudder; machine gun tubes and tubes that would supply heating to those guns and help stop freezing at high altitudes; flaps used to reduce air speed during landing; and the hydraulic shock absorbers known as oleos added on the undercarriage to help cushion the landing. It was now, too, that the Merlin – and later Griffon – engine was installed. The engine was one of a set of primary components that came from outside suppliers – the engine designer Rolls-Royce, based in Derby. The Spitfire factories received a bare engine to which extra features were added by Supermarine's workers. These extras included the support framework for the engine cowlings.

These main assemblies were now ready for the final stage of manufacture and it was at this point that they'd be moved to a new factory. The assemblies would be transported in the early hours of every day to the designated airfields in each factory network – Chattis Hill, High Post, Eastleigh, RAF Keevil, Henley Aerodrome and RAF Aldermaston out in the country. Aircraft were shipped using a fleet of 3-ton (3,000kg), 40ft (12m) trailer trucks designed especially for this unique task. To accommodate the Spitfire, the truck, called a Queen Mary, had a combination of a low, flat floor and loading ramp at the rear with a set of folding, vertical frames along the sides. Within this cradle would sit the fuselage, with propeller attached for transport, and a pair of wings with their undercarriage retracted. It was remarkable that, for all that effort up until now, few workers would see the fruits of their labours completed. 'I never saw a finished Spitfire,' says Joyce. 'The wings were taken away and the next lot brought in.'

Final assembly would see the addition of the windscreen and hood to enclose the cockpit, the connection of motors and sensors to the main column and the pilot's seat installed. The wings were wheeled into position using a trolley and attached to the fuselage, and the heating and cooling systems installed. Waiting to get started on this lot at Chattis Hill was a team that included Joan Burrough. Ten Spitfires would be lined up in two rows of five in the factory, with men and women working on them, seeing them through to completion ready for testing. Joan recalls:

There were all these planes in various stages of being completed. Some were just the fuselage, others would have both wings on or just one. Everybody would be busy with their own job; some at the front, some at the back, some inside. There could be half a dozen around a plane – you'd do your job and move on to the next one.

She was on different jobs – again, setting aside comfort for patriotism and production. 'I had to wash oil filters out in thinners in cold weather. It made you cry – you had no rubber gloves or anything: you'd get chilblains in your fingers. That wasn't very nice.'

Indeed, cold weather was a significant factor. Miles away from the deep countryside and woodland of Chattis Hill, Joyce Hunt worked on wing leading edges at Trowbridge in a facility that, like the Salisbury bus depot, had seen a brick wall partition built in an attempt to separate Spitfire construction from the continuing, pre-war activity. 'We had to have the whole of one wall down and it was freezing – we were in scarves and coats working while they put this wall back. We were going up every two hours to get something from the nurse,' Joyce says.

Back at Chattis Hill, the Spitfire was nearing completion. The final phase was testing and this would ensure that the oil, air, hydraulic and electrical systems all functioned correctly before the propeller was added. Joan says:

> One of my jobs was to wirelock these bits all the way around the propeller. One day I had to more or less put one of these on myself, because the man I was working for couldn't be there. When I saw one of the Spitfires being flown up for test flight, I thought: 'I hope that prop stays on!' Of course, they were all inspected first.

Next, the engine would be tested to make sure all the functions were correctly set. If they weren't, adjustments were made to ensure it was satisfactory for flight test.

> You saw them go up sometimes but that was all – the hangar doors were wide open. You'd hear the engine running – no mistaking that – you'd go down the field and up they'd go. As far as I know they all worked! Sometimes, I suppose there'd be a little fault and they'd come back to put it right, but I can't remember anything serious going wrong.

Thousands of aircraft would be funnelled through final-assembly points such as Chattis, where every completed Spitfire would be put through its paces to ensure it worked as expected. Experimental new craft would be tested, too. That made airfields hubs for some of the company's most important individuals, such as Supermarine's famous test pilot Jeffrey Quill, who would test the Spitfire from prototype in 1936 through to the end of production in 1948 and whom Joan would glimpse only at a distance.

Worthy Down, in the Southampton area, was also responsible for final assembly and experimental work and it became the workplace of a young boy passionate about aircraft, Gordon Monger. On his first visit to Worthy Down, Gordon caught a glimpse of Quill:

> Everybody was rushing around. A Spitfire taxied in through the mud, jumping around and I didn't know it at the time, but that was Jeffrey Quill flying the plane. And then an Avro Anson came in. And I thought: 'My goodness me.' And a lot of men jumped out and rushed around and then the pilot did a 180-degree turn, swung the Anson around and it just missed the hangar door. And I thought: 'Phew, these people are pretty good to swing a plane around like that!'

Spitfire production may have been relentless but Supermarine didn't sacrifice innovation in the drive to greater production and change was a constant factor. Supermarine was engaged in a race against the German military to build the better fighter aircraft. The Messerschmitt Bf 109 would give way after the Battle of Britain to the Focke-Wulf Fw 190, which would prove faster and deliver a new challenge for Spitfire pilots. Later still, the Germans would deliver the first jet-powered fighter aircraft in combat. The race was therefore on for Supermarine to find ways of making successive Spitfire models faster and more responsive. That work took place at High Post, Worthy Down and in Hursley Park's experimental hangar, where designers and engineers refined engines, propellers and wings, modified ailerons and introduced new mechanisms to control the plane.

Quill played his part in this process. He was a force within Supermarine – in direct contact with senior management and with the kind of experience that counted. There from the first Spitfire prototype, he also served during the Battle of Britain so brought a combat pilot's eye view to performance and areas for improvement. In his memoirs, Quill states his personal objective having flown Spitfires against the Messerschmitt:

> The experiences of fighting against Me 109s had, however, made an indelible impression on my mind. The Spitfire's ability to outperform, outfly and preferably out-gun enemy fighters in all circumstances was now, in my view, paramount. Some sacrifice of other qualities in the aeroplane would be acceptable if it were necessary in order to achieve these aims.

Into this slipstream came Gordon. Just a day after his interview, Gordon found himself working at Supermarine in January 1941 as an apprentice fitter erector at Worthy Down before going on to Hursley Park, working on Spitfires and the Seafire naval variant. Aged 16, Gordon was fitting upgraded engines and propellers and performing other modifications on completed aircraft with an assistant two years his junior. He describes how seemingly minor adjustments could make so much difference.

> An aeroplane is very sensitive to these things because it's moving much faster than anything else and a slight change to a panel or the rigging of the aileron can make an important difference to performance. Putting just a small edge of cord on the edge of the aileron, for example, could make a lot of difference.
>
> One day I had this large piece of metal and I was banging up the edges of the aileron and all this lovely filler was flying off. And Alan Clifton, who was head of the technical office, was visiting and he joked: 'We give you these lovely airplanes and look what you do with them!' At the end of the war we tried rods rather than cables through the wings and putting assisted power on the ailerons.

The pace of innovation was astounding. The Spitfire during the Battle of Britain was already a ground-breaking aircraft, but five years of innovation resulted in an aircraft that was faster, more heavily armed, capable of flying further and higher, and adapted to different combat roles. The wonder in all of this, Gordon reflects, was that the design and test team should push the aircraft so far in such a short time, particularly as powered flight had been achieved for the first time just a few decades earlier by the Wright Brothers in 1903. 'Remember the Spitfire was flying very successfully and had completed its life within fifty years of the first ever flight of an aeroplane,' Gordon marvels.

That Supermarine was turning out such wonders at Worthy Down was all the more remarkable given the minimal facilities. Gordon recalls his first morning, arriving by bicycle for a twelve-hour shift starting at 7.30 a.m. one January morning:

> I had to find this hangar and it had no electricity – there was just this one lead lamp. There was no water, no toilets, nothing. It was cold, cold, cold, and in this hangar were a number of Spitfires and they looked beautiful ... We had a pillbox with guns – we didn't really think it was funny but at the time I thought this was a jolly amusing thing.

He recalls the observations that a policeman on guard gave him about Supermarine: 'If you've got a job there my son, you've got a job for life.' He was right: Gordon would go on to serve Supermarine for fifty years.

Supermarine would develop twenty-four marques and yet more variants of the Spitfire. With so many different iterations and with Spitfires produced in such large numbers across such a dispersed area, it was vital that those in the factories knew exactly what to build. Critical to this were the assembly line diagrams that explained how to assemble parts and electronic components. The drawings made by Stella Rutter and others in the Hursley technical publications department were sent to factories inside packing crates of partly produced Spitfires. 'In my group, it was three artist draughtsmen who were doing the assembly drawings and those drawings were given to me to produce on linen for production purposes. Those were the assembly drawings and they were quite different to anything else, and I was the only one who did those,' Stella says.

Stella, a tracer poached from the Royal Navy by Supermarine, was in a highly valued position and working at Hursley meant she mixed with senior management, including chief draughtsman Joe Smith, who became chief designer some years after the death of R.J. Mitchell. She would become a trusted courier by taking messages between Smith and her boss, Supermarine head of technical publications Gerald Gingell. Stella recalls Smith being a quiet, modest person who didn't say much:

I got to know him fairly well, because he'd come down to the drawing office occasionally and asked how I was getting on. I was often given an envelope to take up to the house – it wasn't allowed to go with anybody else, apparently – and I had to walk through the gardens and up to the house and give it to him personally and take back any answer. My job as a postman was quite unusual, because nobody from the drawing office went out to walk up to the office like I did.

The hours for all concerned were long and the work unrelenting but the women of Supermarine's secret workforce found themselves relatively well remunerated. Coming from work in service or retail, where some earned between 6 and 10 shillings a week, wartime pay levels at Supermarine came as a pleasant surprise. And the basic salary was further supplemented with a bonus: Supermarine had taken serious flak from Government officials and the RAF during the early days of Spitfire production for failing to deliver the new planes on time. Bonuses were now just one of the incentives intended to speed things along. Joan at Trowbridge earned £3.50 a week. 'You had so long to do a task and if you did it quicker you got a 50p bonus.' Joyce, also at Trowbridge, had clearly worked so hard during one week of shifts that she thought there'd been a mistake come pay day. 'I had £5 on my check card one week and I put it back. I said: "They've put the wrong card in my box!"' But even this was sometimes trumped by those working on wings

The Castle Road factory today.

at the bus garage: Pat would sometimes hit the heady heights of £10 for a week's hard graft. Despite performing equal work, however, women would frequently find themselves paid less than their male counterparts.

At the end of the day, it didn't matter where in the design, production or experimentation process this workforce served: whether it was drawing, riveting or research and no matter the privations of weather or workload, they poured passion and patriotism into these machines. Nor, it seems, were salary and bonus significant drivers. 'Everybody put their hearts and souls into it, we knew it was for the war,' says Joan Little, working near the start of the Spitfire production line in Trowbridge with her sister, Betty Potter. 'Most of us had husbands, brothers and sisters in the Army, Navy or Air Force – we all put our hearts into it because we knew it was going to help the war. It was lovely. The happiest time of my life. We fell into it lovely. I'd do it all again.'

Joan Burrough, miles away at the other end of the production line in Chattis Hill, had joined because of the proximity of this hidden factory to her family home. She'd heard about the work from a friend who was about to begin there. 'I thought, well you have to do war work, and as it was local I thought I'd apply.' The motivation and camaraderie was a constant. 'I had a brother in the Army,' Joan reflects. 'So you felt you were helping them as well.'

Joyce expands on the family connection of those behind the Spitfire at the secret factories:

We all loved doing our jobs, thinking of our boys in the war. We'd never done it before, and we never knew about aeroplanes, but we all loved it and that made us work. We all knew people's sons or husbands in the Army, Navy or Air Force, so everybody was working to get the war over with quickly.

Everybody was so friendly, there was always a joke going along. You were working for the same thing, being a war on.

BEATRICE SHILLING:
THE WOMAN WHO SAVED
THE SPITFIRE

Of the thousands of women who played their part in Spitfire's story during the war, Beatrice Shilling – nicknamed Tilly – had the biggest impact, introducing a modification to the aircraft's Rolls-Royce Merlin engine that put the hard-pressed pilots of the RAF on a level footing with their German adversaries.

Pilots fighting the Luftwaffe during the Battle of Britain in 1940 had begun to report a small but potentially lethal problem with their otherwise flawless fighter. A design fault meant the

Tilly Shilling: a pioneer in her field.

Spitfire's Merlin engine would cut out if the pilot pitched his plane into a hard nosedive. Such a manoeuvre created negative g-force, causing the carburettor, which controlled the mix of fuel and air, to flood and the engine to stall. RAF pilots were forced to take countermeasures to recover – manoeuvres that exposed both aircraft and pilot to unnecessary risk and gave any Messerschmitt Bf 109 vital seconds in which to escape. Worse, the pilots of the Luftwaffe had become aware of the weak spot in an aeroplane they were struggling to master: a stalling Spitfire released a tell-tale puff of black smoke that the astute adversary could watch for and exploit. Their Messerschmitt Bf 109s did not suffer from the same problem as their engines used a fuel injection system.

It was Beatrice who came to their rescue. She was one of only a handful of women working in aero engineering at the time. Born in 1909 and daughter of a butcher, Beatrice had wanted to become an engineer from an early age and on leaving school gained an apprenticeship at an electrical company run by another pioneer in the field, Margaret Partridge. Margaret was a founding member of the Women's Engineering Society (WES), which had been created to encourage more women to pursue careers in the male-dominated field of engineering. Margaret persuaded Beatrice to apply to study electrical engineering at Manchester's Victoria University, now simply Manchester University, where she was one of just two women undergraduates in her year. Beatrice followed this with a Masters in mechanical engineering.

Beatrice was a pioneer in other ways. She harboured a passion for motorbikes that began at a young age, buying her first at just 14 and joining the motorcycle club at university. Beatrice took up racing at Brooklands in Surrey – the world's first purpose-built motor-racing track. It was during this time she added a supercharger to her machine – hitting 106mph – and was awarded the Brooklands Gold Star for outstanding performance in both track and road racing.

After Manchester, Beatrice landed a job that would change history, at aeronautical research facility the Royal Aircraft Establishment (RAE) in Farnborough, Hampshire. She joined the RAE as a third assistant to the technical publications department but went on to become a specialist in aircraft carburettors, a role that meant she quickly recognised that the answer to the Merlin's stall problem was to develop a system that stopped the carburettor from flooding. Her solution was to insert a small metal disc into the Merlin's carburettor, with a hole in the middle that would help control the flow of fuel and prevent the surge caused by a negative-g manoeuvre. Officially called the RAE restrictor, this device became known by its more colloquial name: Miss Shilling's Orifice. In early 1941 Beatrice and her RAE team travelled to front-line RAF bases to fit the diaphragm. It was an interim measure as Rolls-Royce would modify the engine's design, moving the position of the fuel line and adding a fuel injector to maintain that vital mix of fuel and air. Beatrice would go on to develop a long-term answer to the problem, too, with the RAE Hobson injection carburettor. The remarkable 'Tilly' received official recognition for her invaluable work with an OBE in 1947 and would continue at the RAE until retiring in 1969.

CARELESS TALK COSTS LIVES

There was, it seemed, a piece of Government advice tailored to every aspect of life in wartime Britain. From growing your own vegetables to cutting back on your use of public transport, there existed a campaigning message printed on a poster somewhere. One particular area of focus in the Government's information drive was secrecy: the public was warned to be on guard against revealing too much during conversations, or giving away anything that could be picked up and exploited by German spies or fifth columnists. 'Careless talk costs lives,' Britons were told sternly.

There were few places where the need for secrecy was greater than around Supermarine's new, hidden factories. The dispersal that followed September 1940 had gifted Spitfire production a second chance but with the new production facilities well within the range of German bombers, it was imperative word of their existence should not become widely known.

However, as far as those inside the factories were concerned, it would have been difficult to give the game away had they wanted. The flow of work was non-stop and Spitfire production was defined and repetitive, making it difficult to look beyond one's post to explore the bigger operation. Workers were unlikely to visit the factories outside their own area, while the chances of actually seeing a completed Spitfire were remote, unless they'd been assigned to one of the final assembly airfields, such as High Post or Chattis Hill. Joan Johns, who tested piston rings for Rolls-Royce engines at engineering specialist Wellworthy, testifies to the effects of such total immersion:

> I was completely unaware of what was going on. I suppose people didn't real-ise what was happening and we didn't talk about it. I didn't know anything about it until I went to Wellworthy's and even then it wasn't until after the war that I found out how many aircraft factories there were in Salisbury ... I never remember seeing a part of a Spitfire being taken through the streets. I just assumed they assembled them up at High Post and they were carted around in trucks. But I never saw a Spitfire part.

Joyce Hunt, who built Spitfire wings at Trowbridge, echoes Joan: 'We had no idea where the components went from our factory.'

It was a similar experience for Pat Pearce, also working on wings miles away at Salisbury's Wilts and Dorset Bus Company, who remembers completed

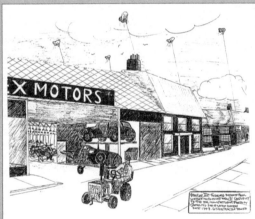

Taking photos would have been seen as espionage but some admirers of the Spitfire kept records. One was Ken Hayter, a local milk delivery boy, who made drawings based on what he'd seen on his rounds during the early morning, before the shutters were pulled down to hide what was behind them.

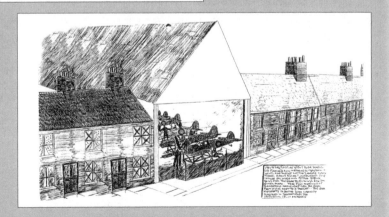

sub-assemblies moving out under cover of night. 'You could see the wings being taken out,' she says. 'We weren't told very much.'

It was not possible to ship all Spitfire sub-assemblies under the cover of darkness but, it seems, even those assemblies that were moved during daylight hours failed to arouse suspicion. One reason was the fact that the factory towns and especially Salisbury had seen an increase in military traffic on their streets into which the low-loader trucks that provided means of transport could simply blend. Another reason was that the Spitfires were difficult to recognise on the back of the trucks, as the fuselage was hidden by its wings tucked along either side.

Bill Edwards, who worked on Spitfires at Castle Road, remembers: 'Every so often, a Queen Mary low-loader truck backed in and they took the fuselage, engine and wings to High Post. In fact they did it in the day, with the parts covered over, and I couldn't believe how somebody didn't twig. They must have seen.'

At the other end of the production line, at airfields including High Post and Chattis Hill, where workers received lorry-loads of sub-assembled wings and bodies to turn into completed Spitfires, the secrecy continued and workers were in the dark over where those components had travelled from. Joan Burrough worked at Chattis Hill, which took fuselages, wings and tail units from the factories around Salisbury. 'I always thought the parts came up from Southampton,' she admits.

The Spitfire was a household name thanks to the Battle of Britain, but employees knew not to discuss their involvement with this by now legendary plane. Even family members were denied the slightest peek. Peter Smith's dad carried out precision engineering in the family home in Reading, making fuel-line parts with a pair of lathes set up in the spare room and then the kitchen – but only once Peter was tucked up safely in bed. Peter sums up the spirit of don't-ask-don't-tell:

> You knew so-and-so was a baker, or that person over there was a butcher, and you knew my father worked for a manufacturing company somewhere, but nobody asked questions about what it was they were doing or why. It was all kept ... well, not hidden but all just out of sight.

'Nobody ever asked [about what we did],' says Trowbridge worker Joan Little. 'We were told not to talk,' adds sister Betty Potter who worked with Joan at Trowbridge. 'We just went to work and came back – and that was that. It suited us fine.'

Secrecy was maintained in part by the Supermarine management, who watched the shop floor closely for signs of over-fraternisation: a quick visit to the toilet was fine, but you risked a reprimand if you dallied en route and engaged in chit-chat. Bill at Castle Road recalls:

They were very cagey. Somebody asked recently how is it we kept the whole operation so secret and I think I know why: everywhere we went there was a poster that said: 'Careless talk costs lives' and you never said a word to anybody. Not even my parents knew what we were doing. I never said a word.

Southampton's fate served as a salutary warning: the fires caused by the bombing could be seen glowing in the night skies from Salisbury, less than 50 miles to the north. Bette Blackwell, working on Spitfires in Wessex Motors, reckoned a good reason for not letting on was nobody wanted their area to suffer a similar fate. Those asking questions, moreover, risked being reported to the police.

This secrecy ran to the very top of Supermarine. Stella Rutter worked in the design offices at the company's relocated headquarters in Hursley Park, the source of each and every new Spitfire design following the dispersal. Based at the heart of design and engineering, and as a key member of a highly skilled team of draughtsmen and tracers, Stella was near those at the very top of the company's chain of command and so interacted frequently with senior management. That meant not just her boss, who was technical publication manager Gerald Gingell, but also chief draughtsman Lovell Cooper and Joe Smith, who became chief designer a few years after the death of R.J. Mitchell. Stella was never tempted to talk about her work or the company:

I knew I was given privileged information and I just kept quiet. I didn't even let my parents know what I was doing. My father never knew anything about what kind of job I was doing, other than I was in a drawing office. I had to keep silent. You worked for the country, not for yourself.

Secrecy became even more important once the US entered the war and preparations for the Allied landings at Normandy with Operation Overlord and D-Day picked up speed. Through her work at head office, Stella fell into the orbit of those masterminding an invasion that would shape the outcome of the war by initiating the liberation of western Europe. Stella was invited to an eve-of-D-Day dance party in the company of US General Omar Bradley, the commander of the US First Army, who was involved in the D-Day planning. She recalls: 'That evening, one of the English girls who'd been asked to come ... was dancing with this American soldier and he suddenly broke down – which was horrendous. Major General Graham dashed across and out the door with the girl and the officer and never came back again.' It was clear the military were not going to risk details of D-Day leaking out at the last minute. 'The girl I knew because she came from Supermarine. I later found out that she had been kept incommunicado for four days to allow the D-Day landings to take effect.'

In the days following the party, Stella found herself fending off questions about the woman's whereabouts and not compromising security by revealing any details.

On the Monday after the party, a very official little man, a union chap, came up to me in my drawing office and asked where she was. I said: 'Oh, she's probably just had too much to drink.' I had to just cover it somehow. He came back to me the next morning: 'Where is she?' he said. 'Even her parents don't know where she is.' Of course I knew, so I had to cover it and just sort of shrug my shoulders. And he came back the next day and I said: 'Go away and leave me alone!' I had to get him off my shoulders ... you had to be very sure you never let anything out that was secret.

Secrecy had become more than just Government advice for those involved with Supermarine – it had become a code of practice. 'The secrecy, and the responsibility of individual people like me, was so important to the progress of the war and we took it as a matter of course,' Stella reflects. 'We knew the secrecy level and you just kept to it for the good of the country.'

FROM PROTOTYPE TO PRODUCTION

BY NORMAN PARKER

The very first Spitfire was wooden – a mock-up. It hung from the roof of Supermarine's experimental department's workshop and helped the company's engineers lay out and build a prototype for testing by Supermarine and the Government. The Spitfire was based on an Aircraft Ministry specification – F37/34 – written by ministry officials to describe the aircraft and that was based on the Type 300 fighter design that had been produced and submitted by Supermarine's chief designer, R.J. Mitchell. The prototype, which would take the serial number K5054, was entirely hand-built, with workers using shaping frames that would form the skeletal foundation of the aircraft and create sub-assemblies. A metal duraluminium skin was rolled by skilled sheet metal workers according to the variable contours and thicknesses of Spitfire's body as set out in the design. These sheets were riveted to the underlying frames, which were all numbered. Bench preparation was an essential part of a Spitfire's manufacture within the secret factory plan, as hundreds of small and larger sub-assemblies could be pre-assembled in relatively small premises before coming together for final assembly at bigger sites.

The tail assembly was attached to the fuselage frame. The fin was an integral part of the tail unit whereas the tailplanes were pre-assembled, separate units, as were the elevators and rudder. The wings – which contained the undercarriage assembly and radiators, machine guns and cannon – became major assemblies in their own right that would be attached to the fuselage with the help of bridging spars. A series of high-tolerance bolts held the wings: each bolt could be enlarged by 0.004 thousand parts of an inch up to a maximum of 0.032, therefore each bolt had its own designated bolt hole for final assembly. The details were displayed on a small plate between the fuselage spar booms. I worked on this and recall great attention to detail was required: we would make holes in a piece of cardboard, into which we placed the bolts when removing the wings so each bolt was removed with its appropriate nut to ensure that when replaced and tightened, a split pin could be inserted.

Prototype was one thing, manufacture was another. The Ministry's initial order for 1,310 Spitfires was the single largest in Supermarine's history and presented the company with a major problem: a factory built to produce relatively small numbers of flying boats simply couldn't handle a production run on this scale. The existing Woolston works were expanded and a new factory was built on land reclaimed from the River Itchen, with work starting in 1938 and the completed plant opening a year later. The Itchen factory became the major production assembly unit supported by Woolston. The maker of wooden seaplanes also had to expand and diversify its base of suppliers, meaning the Spitfire production line was supported by a large number of subcontractors. Not everything ran smoothly. Construction of the wings by subcontractors proved to be a particular problem in the early days, as suppliers struggled with the wings' unique build and many completed fuselages had to be stored, awaiting the arrival of pairs of wings. This contributed to delays that meant Supermarine was unable to deliver its first set of orders on time. Wing production was eventually returned to Supermarine.

UNCLE SAM'S ROLLS-ROYCE ENGINES

The Mk XVI was a little different from the twenty-three other marques of the Spitfire family. Just over 1,000 of this low-level interceptor were built and while it looked noticeably different from those early Mk Is, with a teardrop canopy and low back, it wasn't external design where the essential difference lay. For beating beneath the cowling was a 1,580hp Merlin engine built not by Rolls-Royce staff but the workers of US car giant Packard in Detroit.

Packard, and Ford in Manchester, would be the only two companies outside Rolls-Royce that would be allowed to produce Merlins. These giants of the auto industry had been approached in the belief their industrial muscle could help Rolls-Royce quickly hit the output demanded by the aircraft sector during the war. Merlins weren't only powering the Spitfire, and variants of Rolls-Royce engines would be employed by rivals including Avro, Hawker and de Havilland turning out a plethora of fighters, bombers and multi-role aircraft. Packard-made Merlins would also serve the US war effort, most notably in the Mustang fighter plane.

Of all the suppliers contributing towards the Spitfire, Rolls-Royce was Supermarine's most important partner. Founded in 1906 as a car maker but making aircraft engines for the military since 1915, it was Rolls-Royce pistons that had driven two of R.J. Mitchell's seaplanes to victory in two prestigious Schneider Trophy races

Rolls-Royce engines drove all Spitfires, but Merlins from US car giant Packard powered the Mk XVI.

against planes from around the world. The Rolls-Royce R engine had earned for Mitchell the distinctions of being not just the inventor of the world's fastest plane but also the father of the first aircraft to break the 400mph (643.7kph) barrier. It should have come as no surprise that Mitchell would build the Type 300 that became the Spitfire around yet another promising Rolls-Royce engine, the PV-12, that would become the Merlin.

The war would prove a transformational experience for Rolls-Royce, helping to turn the company into a giant of aircraft engine design. In anticipation of the war, Rolls-Royce had expanded with two new factories in Crewe and Glasgow, but it was the original Rolls-Royce factory in Derby that continued to bear the brunt of development and manufacturing for each new Merlin variant. Operations grew quickly: 2,000 Merlins were produced in the first year of the war but by 1943 that number had broken the 18,000 barrier with the combination of Derby, Crewe and Glasgow as well as Merlin engines from Ford and Packard.

But the job of building Merlins wasn't as straightforward as hoped by those who'd had the idea of turning to the car makers, and Ford and Packard experienced early problems. Rolls-Royce built its engines using skilled fitters who worked with great precision – a process not necessarily compatible with the kinds of rapid mass-production techniques found in the car industry. Ford engineers visited Rolls-Royce in Derby in an attempt to familiarise themselves with the engine drawings and the methods of construction, but reported they could not build the Merlin the same way as Rolls-Royce.

Both Packard and Ford would redraft Rolls-Royce's drawings to suit their own standards and methods. Rolls' aero engine designer Stanley Hooker worked on the Merlins, famously increasing performance by up to 30 per cent. In his book, *Not Much of an Engineer*, Hooker hails the progress that followed: 'Once the great Ford factory at Manchester started production, Merlins came out like shelling peas at the rate of 400 a week. And very good engines they were too, yet never have I seen mention of the massive contribution which the British Ford company made to the build-up of our British air forces,'[19] Hooker says.

Assisted by Rolls-Royce, Packard was able to produce its first Merlins within a year of signing the contract in September 1940. The Packard Merlin was virtually interchangeable in detail with the home-built product, except for the supercharger used to increase performance by increasing air flow: this was a Packard design[20] and would serve in RAF de Havilland Mosquitoes and Avro Lancaster bombers besides Spitfires. A total of 168,040 Merlin engines would be built, with 55,523 from Packard[21] and 30,428 from Ford.

TAKE IT AWAY: TEST PILOTS, DANGER AND THE ATA

To a staff reporter writing on Scottish newspaper the *Daily Record* at the war's end, they were a 'shadow air force', a group of just over a thousand pilots and engineers fulfilling a vital air-support role for the RAF and Royal Navy. This second-line air force ferried Spitfires and other combat aircraft from factories to the front line – anything to anywhere, according to their motto. Theirs was a story of courage, skill and determination; flying in fair weather and foul, risking the dangers of enemy attack without live weapons and making up to half-a-dozen flights each day without radio back-up or sophisticated navigation equipment.

'They' were the civilian pilots of the Air Transport Auxiliary (ATA) whose tireless work earned them the admiration of Lord Beaverbrook, the Government's powerful Minister of Aircraft Production. Although the ATA operated outside the RAF, he hailed them as 'soldiers fighting in the struggle just as completely as if they had been on the battlefront'. Beaverbrook recognised the extent to which the ATA had sustained the RAF during its most desperate hours in the Battle of Britain and beyond, delivering more than 300,000 aircraft across the nation.

Among that 300,000 were many thousands of Spitfires transferred from the airfields serving Supermarine's secret factories in the south of England, and among those pilots delivering these desperately needed aeroplanes were 168 women – the only women permitted to fly aircraft during wartime Britain. They were pilots who would serve with passion and professionalism and, in defying the conventions of the time, would become the first women to pilot the Spitfire. And while in the line of duty they would deliver some of the best-known aeroplanes of the war, from the Hawker Hurricane mainstay of the Battle of Britain to the Avro Lancaster that

The ATA helped keep RAF pilots on the front line.

Eastleigh, near Southampton, was one of a handful of airfields in the secret network where Spitfires were finished and completed aircraft underwent flight testing before they were dispatched.

found fame bombing the dams of the Ruhr Valley and for its night-time raids over the German Reich, it was the Spitfire that left an indelible mark.

Among those ATA pilots was Mary Wilkins-Ellis, who, in her early 20s, had flown sixteen Hurricanes among other aircraft by the time she had her transformative experience in the Spitfire. She would eventually deliver seventy-four Spitfires from Chattis Hill airfield, part of Supermarine's Salisbury-area secret factory network, but recalls the trepidation she felt as she prepared to take control of her very first of the combat aircraft that was quickly building a reputation for power and performance. Adding to her nerves of that first morning was the fact that Mary had been thrown in at the deep end by her controllers at the ATA, who'd ordered that she deliver not one but two Spitfires that day.

'Initially I thought how terrifying it must be to be in a Spitfire because in those days it seemed everyone was saying: "It's a wonderful aeroplane,"' she tells us. Mary wasn't the only one anxious about the prospect of taking the controls of her first Spitfire. 'Someone helped me into the cockpit and I suppose in a way I was nervous and the man from the ground crew who was helping me asked: "How many of these have you flown?" and I said: "None, this is the first one," and he fell backwards onto the ground!'

Once aloft, however, the nerves fell away, as Mary recalls:

I played with a little cloud I saw and I got used to it. The Spitfire was absolutely super and I thought I must land. I had sufficient time to play with the plane and found it was the most wonderful thing that was ever made. It was so light – you just needed a little touch and it would do anything.

Joy Lofthouse thrills at the memory of flying Spitfires and recalls how popular they were among her fellow ATA pilots. 'I did fly a lot of Spitfires – they were delightful,' Joy recalls. 'You practically breathed on the controls and it did what you wanted. It was the nearest thing to having wings. The Spitfire was a lot of people's favourite.'

For Joy, who came from a working-class background, flying Spitfires was a release from the drudgery of life at Lloyds Bank, where she'd worked since leaving grammar school at the age of 16. 'I saw a news item saying the ATA was training new pilots to replace those lost. That sounded much more interesting than working in a bank!'

For Mary, the Spitfire was the ultimate realisation of a girlhood dream, growing up in the shadow of two RAF bases, at Bicester and Port Meadow in Oxfordshire. 'I'd always wanted to fly aeroplanes, ever since I was knee-high to a duck,' she says. 'My father went to Hendon Air Show and initially wanted to take my brothers, but I made such a fuss he took me as well. That cemented my love of flying when

I saw these things,' Mary tells us. 'Later on at school, I was no good at hockey because I was rather small and I didn't enjoy rushing about with these other girls so I was allowed to go to the airfield and learn to fly – I was 16.'

Driven by duty, Mary joined the ATA in October 1941, two months before the Government introduced conscription for women that might have seen her assigned to one of the uniformed branches of the military for women, such as the Women's Auxiliary Air Force (WAAF) formed in June 1939. Had she held out, Mary wouldn't have flown with the WAAF because, while it worked in a range of skilled roles to support the RAF including engineering and maintenance, operating radar control systems and serving as reporters and plotters at RAF bases – a role immortalised in many films – joining aircrew was strictly off limits. 'The war came and I thought that was the end of it, I'll never be allowed to fly again. But I learned from the radio that the ATA needed women because the RAF boys were going to war and there weren't enough people to fly the planes – to transport them from the factories,' Mary says.

That Mary and Joy should get to join this pioneering elite was entirely thanks to another pilot, Pauline Gower. Pauline had been part of a growing movement of women who'd taken up flying during the 1930s, a golden era for the aeroplane typified by adventurers such as Amelia Earhart, who would inspire women to take to the skies. Pauline had flown her own air taxi service and toured with air circuses before joining the British Civil Air Guard (BCAG) as a civil defence commissioner in 1938, where her role was to introduce others to flying through working with local clubs. Flying lessons were expensive but with war coming the BCAG was formed to provide candidates with subsidised training in return for an undertaking that they'd serve in the RAF Reserve if called upon. She switched her attention to the ATA, which had been formed by the pre-war British Airways director Gerard d'Erlanger, and which had a progressive culture, recruiting pilots regardless of age and many physical disabilities but whose first pilots were men. Pauline successfully lobbied for the creation of a women's section, with the first eight admitted to the service on New Year's Day 1940.

The ATA might have opened its doors to women but there were plenty of hurdles left to clear before ascending to the cockpit of a Spitfire. Joy recalls she underwent a 'very tough' medical exam and needed 'certain academic qualifications', of which maths was expected. 'They were pleased I was good at arithmetic,' Joy happily recalls. 'It showed you were well co-ordinated.'

Next came training, at Barton-in-the-Clay, Bedfordshire, and in Thame, Oxfordshire, with recruits put through their paces on single-engine Miles Magisters and Harvards. They were expected to clock up required flying hours by piloting the gnat-like Fairchild Argus and twin-engine Avro Ansons used by the ATA to ferry pilots around the country. Joy says:

We'd fly cross-country making circuits and 'bumps' to do solos. Then you did a secondment to a pool to get the run of the thing – mostly doing taxi work in the Fairchild Argus. Then you came back to the pool and did the same thing again, only this time on a Harvard – so, doing duel flying, solo flying and going cross country.

Flying the single-pilot Arguses and dual-control Ansons wasn't popular, but Joy concedes the value in building up vital flight time and experience for what would come later:

Sometimes you did taxi duty that you didn't like too much but it was very good for your flying because, let's face it, if anything is going to go wrong in your flying it would be in take-off or landing, so you might do six or eight a day, so it sharpened up your flying.

Once qualified, Mary and Joy were expected to be able to fly any aircraft in any of five classes at short notice without necessarily having either seen or flown that type of aeroplane before. The ATA grouped aircraft into six classes, with pilots starting on the most basic Class One, which included de Havilland Tiger Moths used for early pilot training, up through bombers to floatplanes including Short Sunderlands in Class Six that women would not be allowed to pilot. The Spitfire was a Class Two aircraft and training would see pilots introduced to the features and taught the basics of handling and operation. 'There in the corner of the field was the school Spitfire,' says Joy, with a glint in her eye. 'You flew the Spitfire and you were qualified to fly all Class One and Class Two aircraft and you got your wings and uniform and you went to your permanent pool.'

Given the large number of aircraft and the vast array of features and perfor-mance characteristics, each pilot carried with them a copy of the ATA's Ferry Pilots Notes. 'What we had was a loose-leaf folder called Ferry Pilots Notes and that was our Bible. That was 250 types, just a page on each, that told you all you needed to know – take-off, landing, stall,' she says.

'We were taught very thoroughly on all the mysteries of these things,' Mary remembers, 'about variable pitch propellers, hydraulic systems and superchargers because you never knew when you might want it. We were expected to fly all kinds of aeroplanes – fast and slow.'

Like Joy, Mary found Ferry Pilots Notes an invaluable companion. The ATA was expected to ferry American as well as British aircraft, along with some built to serve in the air forces of other Allied nations that would feature some fundamental differences such as units of measurement on the fuel gauge and speed dial. Misreading these could lead to accidents and misadventure. With aircraft

In her early 20s, Mary Wilkins-Ellis had flown sixteen Hurricanes among other aircraft by the time she took the controls of a Spitfire.

Thanks to the pioneering and persistent work of Pauline Gower (here, third from right) skilled women pilots like Mary Wilkins-Ellis and Joy Lofthouse broke through in the ATA.

desperately needed for the fighting forces and with the planes of the secret Spitfire factories produced according to careful planning and design, it was critical not to damage or write off an aircraft through an accident. 'Sometimes the fuel was in gallons and sometimes it wasn't – it was difficult. Sometimes in other planes we were flying on mph and others in knots – that was why the Bible was so efficient because it would tell you beforehand whether it was knots or mph,' Mary says.

Not everything was as well documented as it should have been, though, and nothing could beat swapping tales and sharing intelligence with your fellow pilots, particularly when a bold variant of the Spitfire began entering service with the RAF in late 1942. The Spitfire Mk XII was built partly in answer to the Royal Navy's call for a fighter capable of performing well at low altitudes and it became the first production member of the Spitfire family to feature Rolls-Royce's new Griffon engine. As per requirements, this Griffon-based Spitfire excelled at low altitudes, where it was capable of hitting 372mph (598.6kph) at 5,700ft (1,737.3m) and 397mph (638.9kph) at 18,000ft (5,486.4m). But the Griffon also featured a fundamental engineering change that could catch out the unwary pilot: the crankshaft, which drove the propeller, rotated in the opposite direction to the Merlin. The crankshaft and propeller rotation created a force – torque – that pulled in one direction and to correct this when flying, pilots would pull the tail rudder bar in the opposite direction. The Griffon's crankshaft pulled the Spitfire to the right, but for a generation of pilots used to compensating for the Merlin engine pulling to the left, this went against both experience and instinct, and might have been fatal. The powerful Griffon also demanded the throttle be opened more slowly on take-off, otherwise the Spitfire could move in a severely sideways motion on take-off – dangerous for the pilot and creating unnecessary wear on the tyres. Joy tells us: 'The one nail-biting time I had was when I flew a Spitfire Mk XII or [its successor] the XIV when they went on to the Griffon, and I was told: "Different beast altogether, Joy, open up gently, full opposite rudder to correct the torque."'

The Griffon caught out Mary, too: 'The Spitfire was different, it was a wonderful thing but when they brought in the Griffon engine we were told: "You must be sure to turn the rudder trim to the opposite way it was before. I remembered that, except once where I shot off,"' Mary says.

The new engine wasn't the only challenge the Spitfire threw at the ATA's pilots. The existing duraluminium skin and monocoque fuselage construction made the aeroplane lighter than other aircraft in the RAF fleet and its wheels were comparatively close together. Combined, the light weight and narrow wheel settings would make the Spitfire unstable when taxiing in the kinds of strong head-

or crosswinds that you would typically find sweeping over flat, open airfields. Joy recalls:

> A test pilot once said the Spitfire was a lady in the air but a bitch on the ground because she had a much narrower undercarriage than the Hurricane. So we preferred it if we were on a grass airfield and the caravan could be exactly in the wind and you could wheel her in. But if we had to use the runway and it wasn't into the wind, you had to try and 'three point' her and if you held off the throttle a little too high, you were blown sideways.

This happened to Joy's sister:

> She held off too high and the crosswind got her; she landed hard on the tyre that burst, and she did what we call a 'ground loop' and broke the aeroplane. All she reported was a broken fingernail – she walked away – but she had to go before a court of inquiry that blamed the incident on 'pilot error'. Fortunately they didn't throw her out of the service.

The aircraft's distinctive design could also contribute to it flipping over on the ground in high winds, which led to pilots employing some interesting stabilising techniques – attempts you would be unlikely to see in any newsreels or photos of taxiing Spitfires. The pilot would ask ground crew to sit on the aircraft's tail end to provide additional weight. 'It was troublesome on the ground,' Mary admits. 'You had this great engine in the front so you could not see where you were going and so you had to drive in an S-shape, and we were also always told: "You must have someone sitting on the tail, especially if it's windy and make sure he gets off before you take off!"'

You couldn't always get the volunteers, though:

> One time, I'd asked two or three people: 'Please sit on my tail,' and they'd said: 'No, it was too windy,' but it was a priority plane, and before I could take off it went 'zoomp', like that – over on its nose. Afterwards I was told that no one was to blame because nobody was on my tail.

Pilots' orders for the day came from ATA's headquarters in White Waltham, Berkshire. Pilots were organised into flight pools based across the country, from the south coast near Southampton's Spitfire factories up to Scotland and over to Northern Ireland. The pools at Hamble, Cosford in Shropshire and Hatfield in Hertfordshire would become all-female operations but most saw men and women working side-by-side. Pilots received their flight orders on a piece of paper, or a chit, that specified any number of aircraft they'd be expected to fly that day and their destinations. The Anson or Argus taxis would move the pilots from their pool to collection points such as Chattis Hill, High Post, Keevil or Eastleigh in the secret factory network. Joy enthuses:

> Operations were in Andover and they'd send the list to White Waltham of every aircraft that had to be moved the next day and HQ would dole it out to the pool and try to arrange the transport to get you back – it was a wonderful organisation.
>
> The transport picked you up and took you to the flight office and you went into the restroom and you would pass your time until it was fit to fly. Then a hatch to operations would open and they'd hand out the chitties to what you'd fly – within your class.
>
> When you picked up your chitty, it could be a very varied day. You could just have one delivery and you'd know you'd have to wait there for the taxi aircraft to pick you up, or you'd have one to another place and the nearest pool would come and pick you up and put you someplace else, so you might get two or three during a day, but it would always be within your class.

Planning a route was essential. ATA pilots had been taught to fly without instruments and they initially lacked a radio that would have let them stay in contact with those who might be able to help. They instead relied on their own skills, working with maps in combination with a compass and watch. Mary says:

> We had to know where we were going, so we did an awful lot of map reading because we had no other means of getting from A to B, and that on its own was difficult enough because we had no aids [in the air].
>
> Quite often, one had to get low over the railways and follow the lines. One day I was flying and the weather was bad ... I was following the railway and to my horror the train went into a tunnel and I thought: 'Oh my God, what am I going to do now?' So I kept going for another couple of minutes but fortunately the train popped out again and so I was able to follow it until I got into fine weather. At the time it was rather scary because you were up there and you don't know what to expect.

Pilots studied meteorological reports, too. Weather would pose a problem for ATA pilots, who were instructed to fly at altitudes of just a few thousand feet, meaning they were unable to fly above particularly inclement weather such as heavy rain

Joy Lofthouse on the Spitfire: 'You practically breathed on the controls and it did what you wanted.'

Joy Lofthouse, second row, left-hand side, closest to aircraft, answered the call to join the ATA after seeing a news report while working in a bank.

or storms. This could mean a lot of waiting around in bad weather, so pilots would socialise and pass the time in the restroom area. It was a colourful and mixed environment thanks to the ATA recruitment policy that would see women from more than twenty countries serve. Joy says:

Going in, you hoped the weather would be nice so you could fly. I often thought the rest room at Hamble would make better television than a lot of things. Imagine a gaggle of thirty or forty girls, some talking Polish in one corner, some talking Spanish in another because we had a couple of South American girls.

It was where I learned to play bridge because there was always a bridge school and somebody would have material spread out over the floor and would be cutting out a dress. Then, suddenly the weather cleared, and we had to fly.

Once flying, however, pilots were on their own. Without a radio, ATA pilots had to rely on visual signals from ground crew for vital messages: an Aldis lamp – a portable device used in particular by the Navy at that time for ships to send visual Morse code communications – was used to signal such things as a green all-clear for take-off and landing, or red to relay warnings. Joy recalls the unfettered delight of being in complete control of the Spitfire with just the sound of the engine for company:

They gave you a green when you could take off and red when you couldn't, or didn't have your wheels down when coming in to land, but we didn't have any contact with the ground – you were as free as a bird when you got up there. When you were flying a Spitfire there was no radio – it was total silence. You could just hear the noise of the machine, it felt a part of you somehow, and you were in complete unison with it – it did what you wanted. Nobody to interfere, no voice to override you.

The lack of a radio, however, could pose problems in the event of an emergency, as Mary discovered at Chattis Hill:

I had a Spitfire Mk VIII or IX and I taxied out to the other part of the field and I took off and I couldn't get any green lights so I thought something was wrong. I climbed up to 2,000 feet and I tried everything I could. The airplane was beginning to get rather warm and so was I, and then I couldn't move the undercarriage lever – the lever was stuck and it wouldn't go one way or another – and there was nothing I could do. And I flew around quite a lot up there while on the ground they obviously knew something was wrong, but I couldn't tell them because I had no aids.

Then I saw they'd brought out the ambulance and fire engine and I thought: 'Oh thank goodness, they know I'm in trouble,' and they shot off a green flare to say they were quite prepared for me to crash land. And so it was that I went around again and as I came over the hedge I switched the engine off because I thought that would be a hazard. There was a great crunching, terrible noise and I was almost in tears – I thought I'd broken the aeroplane! People appeared from nowhere, hundreds of them, but I was alright and the aeroplane was not too badly damaged, so it could have been far worse.

Being unable to talk to ground control could be dangerous when coming in to land, too, as there was no way to find out whether the flightpath was clear for approach. 'I flew to Little Rissington, in Gloucestershire, which was terrifying because it was a school and they were flying the twin-engine Oxfords, so I had to fly around and try to find a slot. And I had no aids and as I came down an Oxford came down right in front of me and there was almost a collision,' says Mary.

Barrage balloons, a familiar sight on the wartime landscape floating lazily above cities, factories and other facilities, also presented a challenge. These hydrogen-filled giants ran on average to about 62ft (18m) in length and 25ft (7.6m) in diameter, were anchored to the ground or the back of a truck via a steel cable and floated at a height of up to 5,000ft (1,524m) using a manually operated winch. The goal was to force attacking aircraft to take higher altitudes, reducing their accuracy and bringing them into the range of ground-based British anti-aircraft guns. Ordered to fly at no more than a few thousand feet above the ground, ATA pilots had to be on eagle-eyed lookout for these 'blimps', as they became known.

'Navigation was sometimes difficult because you never knew when barrage balloons were going to pop up, so before you took off you had to find out what the weather was going to be and if a balloon was going to pop up at a certain point,' Mary tells us.

The pilots quickly earned their wings in the Spitfire, but only after a slow start. It was a year and a half after women were admitted to the ATA that they were finally allowed to pilot Spitfires along with other Class Two aircraft, having been confined in the early days to the slow and safe Class One models. That only changed in July 1941 when Pauline Gower, along with a group of other skilled and experienced women pilots, took and passed the exam to fly a Hurricane, paving the way for the first women to fly Spitfires. Mary recalls those early days, before being allowed to fly this most iconic aeroplane. 'I flew Tiger Moths for quite some time because I'd never been near anything else, nor had any of the other girls at that time. It was not a place for young girls, so we were told in those days,' she says.

Lacking radio communication with the ground for support, Mary brought her faulty Spitfire into land at Chattis Hill.

Indeed, some could scarcely believe that a woman, especially one as young as Mary or Joy, could handle the controls of these powerful war planes. Mary recounts one particular incident when delivering a twin-engine Wellington bomber manufactured by Supermarine's owner Vickers, which was designated a Class Four aircraft and on active service would have been crewed by a team of six, including a pilot, radio operator and navigator responsible for flight and control systems. On this particular flight, however, the bomber was flown by a crew of one – Mary. She recounts the reception waiting for her after she'd landed, taxied to a stop and clambered down:

I switched everything off and prepared to get down and there were a lot of RAF chaps outside waiting with a car to take me to the control tower. I opened the door, walked down the steps, and nothing seemed to happen and I said: 'Could we go to the control tower because I have to book in.' And they said: 'We're waiting for the pilot,' and I said: 'I am the pilot,' and they were astonished. They couldn't believe me, so two of them were detailed to go up into the Wellington and they couldn't find anyone. I don't think any of them could ever believe that there was this little girl flying this enormous bomber all by herself.

If flying such mighty aircraft boosted their professional reputations, then their association with the Spitfire would propel them into the national spotlight. To the press, pilots such as Mary and Joy became known as the 'ATA girls' and were featured in newspaper and magazine articles. But these unassuming young women thought they were simply performing their patriotic duty keeping the supply lines of vital aircraft, including Spitfires, flowing while being granted the opportunity to fulfil a personal dream that was taking them in a pioneering new direction.

Pauline summed up what was expected of the women, along with the spirit they brought to the role, telling author Sally Knapp in her book *New Wings for Women* in 1946:

> Flying is a job and like any other should be done by the people qualified to do it. Women in this service were treated exactly like the men, that's one of the things I fought for from the beginning. I have no patience with the type of girl who asks for equal treatment with men, and then, when she gets it, expects special consideration because she is a woman.

Lord Beaverbrook, of course, would go further in his praise for the ATA. He saw them not merely as workers fulfilling a job but, rather, as a force that played a critical role in helping secure the nation's freedom in its support of the RAF. They relieved RAF pilots from the burden of moving aircraft around the country so they could concentrate their attention, and their fire, on the enemy, thereby helping influence the outcome of that most pivotal of conflicts. Without the ATA, the Battle of Britain would have been conducted 'under conditions quite different from the actual events', Beaverbrook reflected years later. In recognition of this, the Government granted the women of the ATA another first: they became the only women in wartime Britain to receive equal pay for performing the same job as men. In those first days of flying with the ATA it had been usual for the women to receive just 20 per cent of the salary of their male colleagues, despite sharing the same qualifications, running the same risks, working the same shifts and notching up thousands of flying hours. In a relatively short time this injustice was overturned, thanks to Pauline's relentless lobbying of the Government and MPs.

For Mary and Joy what mattered most, however, was the opportunity to serve their country while flying. What transformed their duty into something unique was the Spitfire. 'All we wanted to do was fly and fly. I'd have done it for nothing – and yet we were reasonably well paid,' Joy reflects with a smile.

For Mary, dancing across the skies of Britain on those special wings, the Spitfire united the woman in her 20s with the girl from more than a decade earlier who'd been captivated by the sight of her first aeroplane. She confesses: 'The Spitfire in the air was an absolute dream and I often went up and played with the clouds because it was so interesting. I know I shouldn't have done, because fighter pilots were waiting to get these aeroplanes, but I did enjoy it very much.'

LIFE ON THE EDGE:
THE TEST PILOTS' STORY

A generation of pilots revered the Spitfire. No matter if you were an experienced hand or a pilot coming of age, you wanted the Spitfire. Even if you'd never actually seen one, you likely knew the reputation for raw speed and light-touch control. Supermarine's chief designer, R.J. Mitchell, set out to build the ultimate fighter plane and, judging by the reaction, he succeeded.

Playing a critical role in refining his and successive designs were Supermarine's test pilots. Twenty-four marques of Spitfire were designed, plus many more variations, and each had to be put through their real-world paces to ensure they performed at the highest level. As the war progressed, Spitfires became more advanced and as it ended Supermarine looked to a new generation with such new features as a laminar wing in the Spiteful and its naval variant, the

Jeffrey Quill, in the cockpit here with Gordon Monger after the war, flew every Spitfire marque and had a significant influence on development.

Seafang. Test pilots were the designers' eyes and ears in the cockpit, collecting readings and testing a plane's performance while probing for unforeseen problems. Forty-nine test pilots served with Supermarine between 1936 and 1946, working as an extension to the manufacturing process as well as an airborne inspection department. Mitchell placed a premium on their work from the very start, insisting on taking reports verbatim and unedited by his team. Squadron Leader Ralph Sorley, a member of the operational requirements branch of the Air Ministry that had commissioned the Spitfire,[22] would recall: 'He [Mitchell] could talk pilots' language, could understand the pilots' feelings and expressions and, generally speaking, you could get on with him.'

Among those with Mitchell's ear was Jeffrey Quill, only the second person to fly a Spitfire and the individual who would test every variant until the end of production. Few would have the same level of influence over Supermarine's design as Quill, who became chief test pilot but who joined Supermarine's parent Vickers Aircraft somewhat reluctantly. A pilot with the RAF, Quill had applied to become assistant to Supermarine's chief test pilot Joseph 'Mutt' Summers, but had reservations: Quill regarded Vickers as a mundane maker of workhorse aircraft. Fortunately for Quill, and the Spitfire, Summers let on about a forthcoming, high-performance fighter from Supermarine that he'd need help testing. 'This thought cheered me up considerably,' Quill admitted years later. Thus Quill, barely months after joining the company, began a career association with the Spitfire.

Four years after those crucial weeks flying prototype K5054 in early 1936, and with the plane's descendants battling the Luftwaffe, Quill volunteered for front-line duty with the RAF during the Battle of Britain. It was a decision that would help transform the underlying Spitfire design in key areas. Quill succeeded in persuading Supermarine's management to release him for active duty, claiming he would be of more value in the field where he could obtain a pilot's eye view of how the Spitfire handled in action. Serving with 65 Squadron at Hornchurch from 5 to 24 August, Quill shot down a Messerschmitt Bf 109 and Heinkel He 111 bomber in a Spitfire before he was recalled by Supermarine, ostensibly to start testing the Supermarine Mk III. Based on just nineteen days' experience flying and in combat, Quill quickly drew up a list of three areas he felt had to change.

First, the ailerons that controlled direction should be metal rather than fabric. The ailerons' fabric would bulge at very high speeds, disrupting the airflow and helping make the Spitfire harder to manoeuvre; Quill had been left sweating as he tugged on the control stick in the heat of action. He also identified a need to radically improve all-round visibility for the pilot, proposing a change to the shape of the fuselage behind the pilot and also the shape of the pilot's canopy. 'I knew that most pilots were shot down by a Hun they could not see and – having had them on my own tail from time to time – I felt very strongly about the situation.'[23]

He argued, too, for ammunition-round counters but that was not adopted. Flushed by his experiences, Quill said: 'The Spitfire's ability to outperform, out-fly and preferably out-gun enemy fighters in all circumstances was now, in my view, paramount.'[24]

Quill's predecessor as Supermarine's chief test pilot had been Mutt Summers. Regarded as one of the greats, Summers became a test pilot within six months of a posting with the RAF and he progressed to the Aircraft and Armaments Engineering Establishment at RAF Martlesham Heath before moving to Vickers Aviation in 1929

Test pilot Frank Furlong had been a pre-war Grand National champion jockey.

and then Supermarine in 1930. Summers piloted 336 different types of aircraft but it's the Spitfire he's remembered for, taking prototype K5054 up on 5 March 1936. It was a short first flight – just eight minutes – and upon landing and climbing down from the cockpit Summers told the ground crew to leave the aircraft untouched before he took it for a second flight. 'It was a highly successful and encouraging first flight and Mutt Summers, with his experience of flying a great variety of prototypes, was a shrewd judge of an aeroplane,' Quill recalled afterwards. 'I knew him well enough to see that he was obviously elated.'[25]

Of course, flying new and unproven aircraft was a dangerous job where luck played its part. Summers' reputation was founded not simply on the number of aircraft he flew, from the biplane to the jet age, but also on his ability to extricate himself from tight situations. Summers had a number of close calls before and during his time at Supermarine. As for luck, three years after Summers and Quill piloted prototype K5054 it suffered an in-flight drop in oil pressure and crash landed. Pilot Flight Lt Gilbert Standage White died later from injuries he sustained.

Supermarine's Hursley House team designed and refined the planes that Quill, Furlong and others put through their paces ahead of production.

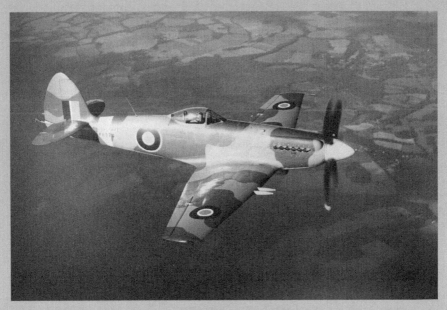

The Seafang.

Fate shadowed Quill years later, too, while putting the Supermarine's planned successor to the Spitfire, the Spiteful, through its paces with colleague Frank Furlong, who was operating from the High Post and Chattis Hill airfields that were part of the Salisbury network of secret Spitfire factories. Quill had recruited Furlong from the Royal Navy, where he'd flown the carrier-borne fighter/reconnaissance Fairey Fulmar and played a part in the dramatic sinking of the *Bismarck* in May 1941. Furlong had shadowed the German Navy's feared battleship before his plane was forced to ditch in the North Atlantic, from where he and his fellow crewman were rescued.

Unlike Quill or Summers, Furlong lacked an engineering background, having raced horses before the war and won the Grand National, but he was clearly gifted and had studied hard. One day in September 1944, Furlong took Spiteful prototype NN660 for a test flight. Among the features that differentiated the Spiteful was the use of then-new push-pull control rods to operate the ailerons rather than the cables running over pulleys. As Furlong returned to High Post, he engaged in a mock dogfight with a Spitfire Mk XIV. While going very fast and at low altitude, Furlong's plane flipped onto its back and, before he could recover it, hit the ground in a valley, killing him.

Quill would later have his own struggle against a Spiteful when the aileron of the prototype he was flying jammed during a high-g-force turn. Quill eased off the speed and claims to have given the joystick a 'mighty wallop' with the palm of his hand to knock the aileron free and recover. Quill, who'd been at a higher altitude than Furlong, suggested Furlong's death was the result of the new control system jamming rather than pilot error. It was a sobering reminder of the stakes involved and the role of fate for Supermarine's test pilots.

ONE IDEA, 24 MARQUES: WELCOME TO THE VERSATILE SPITFIRE

BY NORMAN PARKER

More than 20,000 Spitfires were produced in the twenty-four different models and an additional number of variations. The different types of Spitfire were each allocated a marque (Mk) number. Production began with the Mk I, which used a Merlin II or III engine, and the Mk number changed as new models were produced, usually with a modification in design or engine, operational role or weapons. Different variations would have a suffix letter such as an A, B, C, D or E that reflected the change. For example, the letter 'A' referred to the original wing design with eight .303 calibre Browning machine guns, while a 'B' suffix denoted two 20mm Hispano cannon and four Browning machine guns and so on. Alongside these advancements came photographic reconnaissance versions, where all machine guns were replaced with cameras and the wings' leading-edge structure would house fuel tanks along with the cameras – this was a 'D' class of wing while the photo reconnaissance Spitfire became established in production as the PR. A number of Mk IIs were modified for air-sea rescue to become the ASR Mk 2C with a valise that carried a rescue dinghy behind and below the cockpit, to allow speedy assistance for a pilot downed in the sea. Such modifications made operating an already complex aircraft more complicated as each Spitfire type and marque entering production was different from the initial design. Each Spitfire therefore required something called a build standard, which was a set of technical drawings and a list of components that would help when it came to ordering spares for maintenance, repair and modification.

Some variations had an extremely short production run. The Mk III, for example, was intended as the next design progression to be built around the Merlin 60 engine series, with a two-stage, two-speed supercharger, but just two were built. It was overtaken by the Mk V. The Mk IV, meanwhile, saw just two airframes built and powered by Rolls-Royce's successor to the Merlin engine, the Griffon. One of these became the prototype Mk 20 and the other the prototype Mk 21.

The PR Mk IV, with Merlin 45/46, was the production version of the PR D developed from the Mk V with armament replaced by leading-edge fuel tanks, hence the 'D' identity. Introduced in October 1940, it had the longest range of any of the early Spitfires thanks to 114 gallons (518.2 litres) of fuel in the wings, giving it a maximum range of 2,000 miles (3,218.6km).

Supermarine was in a race against the Luftwaffe to produce aircraft capable of flying faster and higher. From this race came the Mk VI, a high-altitude interceptor equipped with a pressurised cabin and featuring elongated wings to enable it to perform at up to 39,000ft (11,887m). It was Supermarine's response to the perceived threat of high-level bombers, such as the Ju 86, which never actually materialised.

The Mk VIII was intended to be the next design step based on the progressive development of the Mk V, VI and VII but was overtaken by the Mk IX with the installation of the Merlin 60 series engines in a Mk VC airframe. The IX was produced in vast numbers – more than 5,000 between October 1941 and April 1944, making it second only to the Mk V in output.

The Mk V became an early staple in the battle against the Luftwaffe, outperforming German aircraft for speed and manoeuvrability, but the tables began to turn in the Luftwaffe's favour with the arrival of the Focke-Wulf Fw 190. The Spitfire Mk IX was the RAF's response, using the Merlin 60 and 70 series engines of a Mk VIII but in a modified Mk VC fuselage. It was a significant improvement over the Mk V: a top speed of 409mph (658kph) at 28,000ft (8,534m), an increase of 40mph (64kph), and a service ceiling of 43,000ft compared with 36,200ft (11,033m).

Hursley Park, seen today, the cradle of Spitfire design.

The experimental hangar at Hursley Park, where innovation in design and engineering became real.

In August 1941 the Mk XII saw the full-scale introduction of the Griffon engine that delivered greater power and performance and this marque, with its clipped wings, was built to serve as a low-level interceptor. This brand new engine was based on the Rolls-Royce R engine that had powered the Supermarine S.6B racing seaplane that won the Schneider Trophy for Britain in 1931. The Griffon would power all subsequent developments of the Spitfire. However, it featured a crankshaft and propeller rotating in the opposite direction to the Merlin, changes that created some difficulties for those Spitfire pilots raised handling the earlier generation of Rolls-Royce engine. Just 100 of the Mk XII were built – all in Salisbury.

The Mk XIV built for the fighter and fighter-reconnaissance role was simply a Mk VIII with the Griffon engine. An increased engine length saw the introduction of lead ballast weights in the rear fuselage to maintain its centre of gravity, a ploy used elsewhere in earlier Spitfire design. The fuselage was built in two versions: the standard cockpit installation and later versions that saw the rear fuselage reduced in height to the same level as the fuel tank and a one-piece, rear-view sliding canopy fitted with an improved profile that included a hood winding gear to help overcome forward air pressure.

The Mk XVI was a Mk IX fitted with a Merlin from US car-maker Packard, making it a Mk IX or XVI depending on the type of engine fitted. As with other engines, the Packard version of the Merlin required its own series of Air Publications, published information covering such activities as repair and modifications and performance instructions. The Air Publications for the Packard Merlin took on an added significance because of the different build standards. Both of these, like the Mk XIV later versions, saw the installation of the low back and rear-view canopy. The Mk XVIII replaced the Mk XIV and featured strengthened wings and main undercarriage to enable it to carry 60lb (27kg) rockets that would be slung below the wings. Like the Mk XIV, the Mk XVIII operated in the attacking and fighter/reconnaissance role. It was a Mk VIII with the Griffon engine.

The Mk XIX was an incredible member of the Spitfire family: based on the Mk XI but with the Griffon engine of the Mk XIV, it was built for photographic reconnaissance. A tank capacity of 256 gallons (1,163 litres) – three-and-a-half times that of the original Spitfire – a top speed of 460mph (740.2kph) and a pressurised cabin, meant it remained in service into the 1950s, long after mainstream Spitfire production had finished and well into the age of jet power.

The Mk 21 – note the change from Roman numerals – had a similar fuselage to the later Mk XVIIIs but came with a brand new wing, a culmination of the developments in design since 1934, which featured a fully enclosed undercarriage. The Mk 21 used either the two-stage, super-charged Griffon 61 engine with a five-blade propeller, or a Griffon 87 driving a six-blade propeller that was carried on into the Mk 22 and 23.

SPITEFULS AND SEAFIRES

The Supermarine Spiteful was an entirely new design from Supermarine's chief designer Joe Smith and his team. Not too dissimilar to the Spitfire in outline, the familiar elliptical wing had given way to an angular-shaped laminar flow design and the narrow undercarriage track was replaced by a wider, inwardly retracting unit. The armament remained the same: four 20mm Mk V cannon, but with two 1,000lb (453kg) bombs and four 300lb (136kg) rocket projectiles. The cockpit area was raised to improve the pilot's view over the 2,375hp Griffon 69 engine and it had a larger tail unit. However, the design changes proved pointless as there was little improved performance on the Mk 24. Just twenty Spitefuls were built – seven as test aircraft, six tested and flown and seven completed, not flown and sold as scrap.

At the start of the war, the Royal Navy's Fleet Air Arm lacked a comparable fighter to the RAF's Spitfire. Design development had been restricted to such a degree that the fleet's relatively small aircraft carriers could not protect themselves from a modern air attack. The Spitfire or the Hurricane were the obvious contenders and a Mk I Spitfire was passed over to allow Navy pilots to get to know their modern mounts. Two Mk IA Spitfires would be converted and strengthened to carry an A-frame deck-arresting hook below the rear fuselage with three 27lb (12.2kg) weights attached to the engine bearer to compensate for the additional weight of the hook. Those with deck-arresting gear became the Seafire Mk IB and those with catapult spools the Mk IC.

The Seafire Mk IB was a converted Spitfire Mk VB and the Seafire Mk IIC a converted Spitfire Mk VCs, with many of the Mk IICs built in the factories around Salisbury. Manually folding wings were introduced to the Seafire with the Mk III, paving the way for this to become the standard fighter aircraft of the Fleet Air Arm throughout the war. Variations and improvements would follow, including the introduction of the Griffon to the main Spitfire line, performed with the Navy in mind. The follow-on Seafire Mk XV, XVII, 45, 46 and 47 were naval versions of the Spitfire Mk XV, XVII, 21, 22 and 24 respectively.

Full list of all the Spitfire marques:

Prototype K5054	Mk XI
Mk I	Mk XII
Mk II	Mk XIII
Mk III	Mk XIV
Mk IV	Mk XVI
PR IV	Mk XVIII
Mk V	Mk XIX
Mk VI	Mk 20
Mk VII	Mk 21
Mk VIII	Mk 22
Mk IX	Mk 23
Mk X	Mk 24

THE SPITFIRE IN PIECES

BY NORMAN PARKER

Supermarine's Type 300 was a relatively straightforward concept: a day and night fighter built to the Air Ministry's specification – albeit a specification adapted to R.J. Mitchell's aircraft.

Developing the Spitfire was a finely crafted collaboration between architect and builder. A chief designer would decide the final shape and layout of their new design, which would then move into the hands of the design teams, who would produce more detailed designs and drawings for the structure to support the shape. Stress and weight distribution engineers would then agree on the limitations afforded by the available space while also working within constraints of cost and weight. Any one of these constraints could affect the final performance, resulting in certain Spitfire marques and types that were superior in form and function.

The next stage was to produce a vast number of drawings that production teams could use for final assembly. It was now that problems unforeseen on paper could appear. These were often resolved by the fitter, who'd make difficult parts fit, with the drawing redone accordingly. The next stage in development was the assembly of the basic components into sub-assemblies, produced in their thousands, that would combine to produce the final design. Take the fuselage: this consisted of a series of frames that were made of two half-frames joined together at the top and bottom. Each frame was a different size and had to be assembled into the fuselage jig – a type of frame built for the construction of sub-assemblies into a final assembly – at the requisite position. Hundreds of fuselage frames could be pre-built for mounting in the fuselage jig, ready for skinning. The same applied to the wing and tailplane ribs.

Each frame was given a number identifying its position in the jig. The Spitfire fuselage frames began with frame number five, with frame numbers one to four being the structure forward of frame five and supporting cowlings surrounding the engine and propeller. Frame five was the most important of all. The lower section carried the bridging spars to which each wing was attached and its upper structure formed a fireproof bulkhead between the engine and fuel tanks. This crucial frame also carried the engine's weight load and thrust that were transmitted rearwards via four longerons – longitudinal, load-bearing framework components attached to the fuselage structure.

Spitfire manufacture was an extremely complicated process and not readily suited to the kinds of massive scale production lines of other aircraft. Building just thus far would have clocked up hundreds of people hours and considerable costs. Ultimately, it would take 15,000 person hours to build the Spitfire, versus just 9,000 for the Hawker Hurricane. This helped contribute to the fact that more Hurricanes were initially built during the RAF's early rearmament. The small component-based nature of the Spitfire, however, lent it to construction in smaller factories producing sub-assemblies, whereas the Hurricane required fixed factory space.

The wings followed the same principle as the fuselage, although layout was completely different. The main spars began life as lengths of circular, high-strength telescopic tubing. These were re-formed into square sections that became progressively smaller towards the wing tips. The wing tips could be removed to help reduce the span and increase the roll rate for low-altitude operations or left in situ for normal operations. They could even be extended by 3ft to increase the span for high-level operations. This build flexibility could be combined with a range of engine types to suit these specialist functions.

The following diagram and photos walk you through the Spitfire's sub-assemblies and fundamental features.

KEY (SEE DIAGRAM OVERLEAF)

1	R.J. Mitchell broke with aircraft manufacturing tradition when he conceived the Spitfire, to deliver a breakthrough in engineering and design.
2	Nineteen duraluminium frames – all numbered – formed the fuselage's skeleton and gave the Spitfire its distinctive shape.
3	Duraluminium skin and frames were joined to build a monocoque structure that ensured a strong, compact and lightweight aircraft.
4	Rather than fabric, Mitchell made the Spitfire's skin from sheets of stressed duraluminium that had been formed in different thicknesses.
5	The monocoque construction transferred flight stresses to the metal frame and skin, doing away with the need for a maze of internal beams and supports that strengthened earlier aircraft.
6	The cockpit was one of three sub-assemblies – with engine and aft sections – that when combined made up the fuselage.
7	The tail-fin unit was built as its own assembly.
8	Rolls-Royce's Merlin and Griffon engines supplied the horsepower, with top speeds at different altitudes gradually increasing as the war progressed.
9	Engines were added to the Spitfire's fuselage before everything was transported to a designated airfield for final assembly.
10	Like the fuselage, wings were built using sub-assemblies but could be adapted to suit specialised combat roles.
11	Wing sections were combined in a jig for further work, with such things as bays added to the underside for the engine radiator and retraction of the undercarriage.
12	The Spitfire Mk IA debuted with eight 7.7mm wing-mounted machine guns and the Mk IB four machine guns and two cannon, but as the war progressed and wing design evolved, marques gained more options, including the capability to carry bombs.
13	Wing, fuselage and tail unit sub-assemblies were all cleaned before being primed and painted in the RAF's familiar camouflage colours.

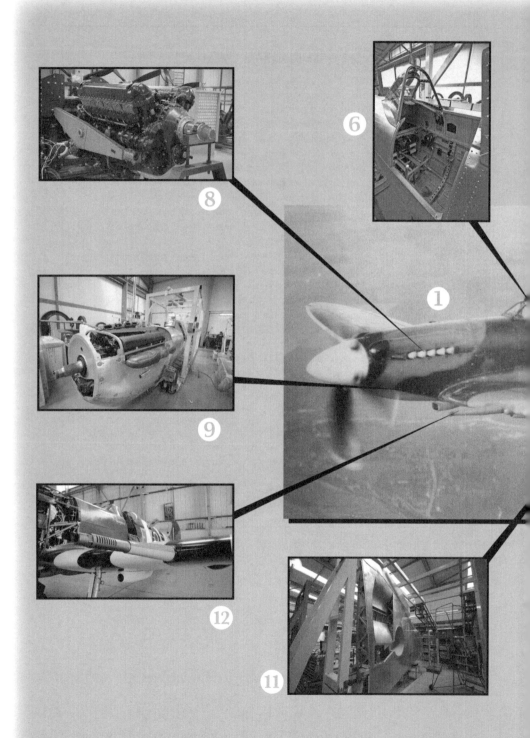

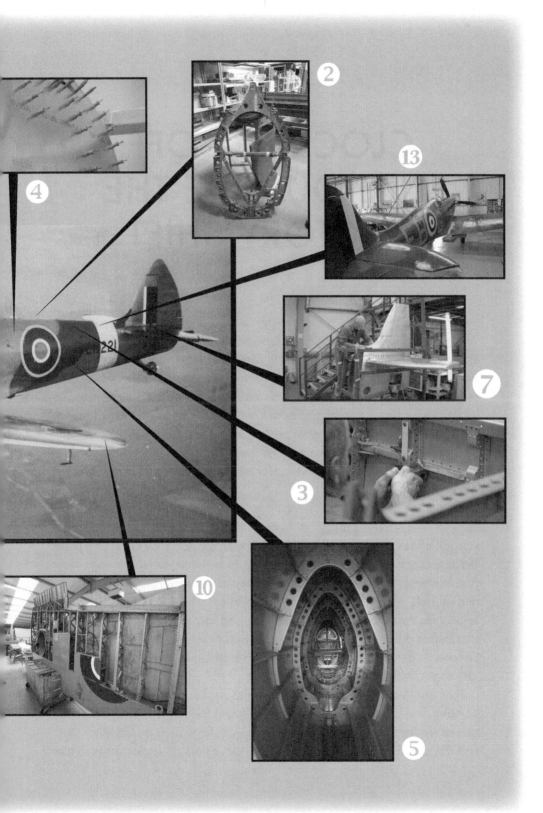

CLOCKING OFF: LIFE OUTSIDE THE FACTORY SHIFT

'I have nothing to offer but blood, toil, tears and sweat,' Winston Churchill told the nation upon becoming Prime Minister in May 1940, eight months after the start of the war. Toiling on twelve-hour shifts, 365 days a year, the hidden army behind secret Spitfire production would become the living embodiment of that spirit. 'They would clock on in the morning and be in that building until late at night,' according to former Vickers Supermarine engineer and Spitfire historian Norman Parker. 'You had a break for meals and a cup of tea, but it was mostly in the working area. You might have to walk down the road for that cup of tea but it was all contained around the production site.'

Life outside that schedule offered limited diversion, too, and there were few areas of these workers' personal or domestic lives where the war did not encroach. Hungry, following that long shift, there was little satisfaction to be found on a plate. The impact of the war in the Atlantic was felt on the dinner table with eggs, meat and other staples rationed by the Government to ensure enough for everybody and officials offering tips on ways to supplement meals using bread and root vegetables. Fresh fruit was difficult to obtain, and fare such as bananas, oranges and lemons disappeared. Even the simple act of freshening up following a shift became harder the longer the war lasted, with the Government introducing soap rationing in 1942.

Then there was the ever-present worry that you or your loved ones might be bombed. The Luftwaffe switched from pounding London in late 1940 to trying to weaken Britain's capacity to wage war, with huge raids on industrial cities and docks and bombers nightly unleashing clouds of high explosives to shatter buildings, followed by incendiary bombs to consume the remains in fire. You didn't need to be directly beneath the bombers to feel the effects, as the residents and Spitfire-factory workers of Salisbury discovered: looking out at night they'd see the sky over Southampton, just 23 miles (37km) to the south, red from the fires of the bombs. On your radio, meanwhile, you could listen to German propaganda threatening that your area was next.

Sometimes the Luftwaffe did strike, as when a pair of Focke-Wulf Fw190s swooped in on a low-level, daytime raid over Salisbury that would send those caught out in the open diving for cover as the fighters raked the ground with gunfire. Gordon Topp was the telegram boy whose working days were spent diligently criss-crossing Salisbury delivering messages and who – as a civilian – was lucky enough to peek inside the city's secret Spitfire factories on his rounds. Gordon sets the scene of the raid that took place during one of his many shifts: 'I was in the post office on Chipper Lane, off Castle Street, looking out the window and I heard a roar as they came across the market square.'

Local girl Adele Stokes, who was in her early teens, had been sent by her mother to fetch her younger brothers for tea when the raiders struck, machine-gunning those on the ground. She recalls:

I was crossing the road and I saw this aircraft coming down and swooping towards us and I thought: 'He's a German,' I just knew he was going to do something. Luckily there was a hedge and I threw my two brothers on the ground and jumped on top of them, squashing them with my arms, as the pilot machine-gunned up the road ... I felt sure they were meant for us.

The aircraft flew low enough for those on the ground to make out details of the pilot. 'There was this plane flying over the top of the trees,' says another resident, John Bletsoe. 'Dad saw German markings on it, he grabbed us, threw us down on the grass, and sprawled himself on top of us. We were facing towards the plane and if you looked up you could see the pilot and his light-coloured helmet.'

Their target was the city's big utility, the gasworks run by the Salisbury Gas Light and Coke Company. One Fw 190 dropped a single bomb nearby, on Middleton Road, and unleashed a hail of bullets on one of the two gasometers in the hope of sparking a devastating blast. Local boy Ray Elliott describes what happened next:

At zero height, or so it seemed to me, was this plane coming in very slowly, you could see the pilot, his helmet, his goggles, and I said: 'Look something's fallen off. Hey, it's got a black cross on it – I've never seen one of them before,' then

Living near Salisbury's gas works and alone at night, Hilda Mitchenere feared the sound of the German bombers overhead.

Hilda's father risked his life to repair Salisbury's gas holder following a direct hit on the gas works by Luftwaffe raiders.

orange flames shot out the leading edge of the wing, going bang, bang, bang. And I thought: 'That's one of theirs!' And we soon found out what had fallen off – there was an enormous explosion on the other side of the railway line.

Crossing under the railway bridge that traverses the road, Ray emerged to witness the aftermath. 'There was a knot of people looking at the gas holder and in the side was a hole belching flames – massive flames – 10ft [3m] high I should think.'

The fire brigade was soon on the scene but it took the bravery of one man to contain the escaping gas – the father of local resident Hilda Mitchenere, who climbed a ladder to patch the hole. She tells us:

When the siren went, I dived into a little shop immediately, and I was very, very worried and I dashed home and my husband had already come down to the gasworks to find out what had happened. My father was halfway up the gas holder mending the holes with the fire engines constantly spraying water on him to stop any fire. He was quite some time until the early hours of the morning and went home with a completely wet suit.

Attacks by the Luftwaffe on Salisbury weren't confined to gasworks, and the presence of a train station and depot marked out the city as a convenient target. Local boy Roy Fittall recalls another daring low-level raid:

We saw this aeroplane coming up the railway line and one of the boys in our group started waving to it but another, Edwards, who was an evacuee from London, he said: 'Get down, that's a German!' We said that's not a German plane coming up the railway line, but it was and he came in low. You could see the German in there, large as life – the tail gunner – and we flattened ourselves against the wall. We heard a rat-a-tat-tat and he was machine-gunning the railway sheds. He didn't get much further because a Spitfire brought it down just out of Salisbury. Turned out this London kid recognised the plane as a Dornier. Coming from London, he'd probably seen them overhead.

Reading, some 60 miles (96km) to the east, would also succumb. Reading was something of a target thanks to the presence of a major railway line through its centre with a station that, unbeknown to the Germans, happened to be in close proximity to a covert Spitfire factory at Vincents Garage, home to fuselages and sub-assemblies. A line of bombs dropped one day would miss Vincents but cause death and destruction nearby. German bombs would also strike the domestic Spitfire 'factory' of Peter Smith's dad at Caversham to the north. Aged just 4 at the time, Peter recalls the impact of an incendiary bomb attack on the family home:

We were sitting in the kitchen and there was a big bang at three o'clock in the afternoon and mother looked out the window and saw these flames coming out of the ground. She'd been told by my father it was probably an incendiary device and the thing to do was throw a bucket of sand on it. It was near my sand pit, and I remember peeking around my mother's skirt as she was shovelling sand on these flames and they went out.

She decided to check on the neighbours and mum went to get her coat from behind the door of the front room. As she opened the front-room door, a big cloud of dust came out because a bomb had gone through the roof into the bedroom upstairs, blowing out the windows and bringing down the front-room ceiling. She grabbed her coat and ushered me outside quickly to see what was going on and we could see these various little fires down the road, which were left to burn themselves out.

The calm of Trowbridge was shattered one July morning in 1942 as workers were heading to their early shifts. A hit-and-run raider scored a direct hit on the British

Legion Club – now known as Bridge House – killing two and reducing the Bear Pub opposite to a single storey. Local boy Stanley Jones recalls:

> We were still in bed. Maybe the sirens had gone and we were just a little complacent but I say to this day I am not quite sure whether I was blown out of bed or jumped out very quickly. As the bombs were about a quarter of a mile away, perhaps it was the latter, but I remember my mum dashing to the bedroom window and saying: 'That one was close ...'

The damage was minor but could have been worse. Stanley continues:

> After school we went to have a look at the devastation. What was most dramatic was the huge crater at the gasworks gate. One of the bombs had only just missed the large gasometer. There was another crater behind Hill Street close to the river ... small groups of older folk wandered around not quite believing that this could have happened in their own town.[26]

The Luftwaffe would eventually strike all the major centres harbouring secret Spitfire factories but as part of the broader bombing campaign rather than a deliberate strategy to hit these unique facilities tucked away inside garages, factories and other ordinary commercial buildings and homes. The dispersal plan worked and Hitler's aerial campaign over Britain failed to dent output of his Air Force's nemesis, with 12,000 Spitfires delivered. Had the German command known about these factories, it would inevitably have intensified the raids.

It seems the Germans were equally unaware of the presence of thousands of US troops in one of those places hiding the Spitfire factories: Salisbury saw a staggering build-up of soldiers ahead of the Allied landings in Normandy, France, in June 1944 that would begin the campaign to liberate Europe. US troops, known as GIs, were stationed in Salisbury and the surrounding towns and villages up to 30 miles (48km) away in order to position them for training on Salisbury Plain and as part of a massive plan of deception to keep them hidden from German spies and aerial intelligence ahead of what would be the largest combined military operation in history.

Salisbury became a hub of D-Day preparation. US and British commanders General Eisenhower and Field Marshal Bernard Montgomery and others joined Churchill there for meetings, US Army commands established HQs at stately homes and manor houses around the city, and the US Army built a 1,000-bed hospital at Odstock under its 5th General Hospital Unit to care for injured US troops. With them, too, came a branch of the Post Exchange (PX), an organisation selling merchandise and offering recreational facilities to US troops. It was thanks to the PX on Silver Street that items such as fruit, ice cream, doughnuts, chocolate, nylon stockings and cosmetics – rationed or difficult to obtain for the ordinary Brit – would find their way into the hands or on to the dinner tables of the locals of Salisbury. Air Transport Auxiliary pilot Joy Lofthouse recalls:

> You knew the food was good. It was better than ours and they'd take you to the PX – the equivalent of our NAAFI [the Navy, Army and Air Force Institutes] – and let you buy lipstick and stockings and things like that, so the Americans were very popular in one way.

For Bette Blackwell, punching rivets into Spitfire after Spitfire at Wessex Motors, it was the doughnuts sold near the hospital that stood out: 'They used to have a van outside selling their doughnuts. They were lovely!'

The PX and the hospital became hotspots for dances that, for the women in the Spitfire factories, became a great way to unwind and briefly forget the worries of the war to the latest big band sounds of Glenn Miller from across the Atlantic. A devoted dance fan, Bette recalls cycling distances of up to 30 miles for weekly dances and making it to special events such as Halloween. Cycling wasn't necessary to get to the US Army's events, however, as they would lay on transport. 'They would put on a big truck to pick us up and there were always two of them on that truck to make sure none of them interfered with any girls ... I wasn't short of boyfriends and they taught me to Jitterbug quite quickly because I liked ballroom dancing,' she says.

Joyce Hunt, who worked in the Trowbridge area, recalls the release of the dance floor. 'My husband was a prisoner of war for four years and we hadn't been married that long. But as for talking about it, that never entered your mind. We just went dancing. I loved dancing. When you were in a place like that you didn't think of our work, because it was our outlet,' she says.

The atmosphere was one of energy and fun. Pat Pearce, building Spitfire wings at the premises of the Wilts and Dorset Bus Company in Salisbury, recalls few concerns about mixing with so many soldiers from overseas. The same could not be said of Pat's dad, with three daughters. She explains:

> We could go to the dances and you never heard of anything nasty going on. But it was a bit of a worry for those who had daughters. My dad had three to think about and he couldn't go to sleep until we were all in. He'd get in and out of bed to see where you were. He went all up the garden to see where I was one night and mum said: 'What are you getting in and out for?' and he said: 'Well Patti's

in bed, Barbie's in bed but I don't know when she crept in' – they worried more than what the mothers did!

Of course, night shifts made dancing difficult. 'We used to envy those people who never had a go on night work,' Pat says. 'We started saying: "Let's make out we are not very well."' Somebody told the factory's little chargehand ... and when he caught us, it was terrible. "Is there something on out that way on a Thursday night, that you are not very well?" he asked. We didn't know whether to laugh or cry.'

Dancing could get you into trouble in other ways, too, as Pat discovered returning late one night by bicycle from the village of Bolford, 11 miles away, without the identity papers you were expected to carry and show when asked by officials. She might have been earning a decent wage working on Spitfires for the war, but for Pat at home with her parents it was Dad who continued to rule the house. Pat recalls:

> We went along the back road, the three of us. A policeman lived along the back road and he saw us without any lights and he stopped us and said: 'Where's your identity cards?' We didn't have our identity cards. He said bring them along to the station tomorrow morning. We didn't know what to do – we were frightened to death, our dad was so strict. Well the next week it was all in the paper. Mum knew about it but Dad didn't and this bloke who worked with our dad said: 'Freddy, I see your daughters were fined last week for going along to Bolford without any lights.' He said: 'First I've heard about it.' My God, didn't he go on.

The US Army brought international celebrities to Salisbury, too. Among them, world heavyweight boxing champion Joe Louis, an army sergeant assigned to entertaining the troops and who would perform at boxing matches in the field. Louis was a major attraction: on the road to his title he'd taken on German rival Max Schmeling in a match pregnant with ideological tension and national rivalry. Schmeling had beaten the up-and-coming Louis in 1936 but in a rematch two years later Louis had his revenge. Schmeling was not particularly political and had refused to join the Nazi party, but the Nazi machine sought to extract maximum political advantage from the match against the 20-something African–American Louis, whose nickname was the Brown Bomber. Louis would knock out Schmeling early, sending his opponent to the hospital in a match broadcast live on the radio from New York's Yankee Stadium. The young Ray Elliott was left speechless at the sight of this international sensation in the ring at Salisbury's Victoria Park. 'You could see a platform up above the heads of the crowd and there were two people in there. And I wondered what they were doing and I asked a chap. "Boxing match,' he said. "We've got a special guest today – Joe Louis." I said: "What, the heavyweight champion of the world?" and he said: "Yes, he's a sergeant in the army."'

Glenn Miller also performed a concert that generated an audience from far and wide. The music of Miller and his famous orchestra would help define the soundtrack to the war, with fans stomping and swinging in halls across the land to hits such as 'In The Mood', 'Moonlight Serenade' and 'Chattanooga Choo Choo'. Among his legion of fans was Bette. She tells us:

> My friend May Skeets was mad on Glenn Miller like me and he was on at Victoria Park in Salisbury. They had one entrance and the guards there. We had these two tickets. We got to see Glenn Miller in the distance because there were hundreds and thousands of Americans – they'd come from all over the country to see him. It was the first time I'd seen a band with their cornets swing from side to side.

Then there was sport, too. Bette remembers:

> I was mad on dancing. I didn't play much sport, only football. We had a ladies' football team during the war, with single girls versus married, six-a-side. I can remember playing against the Army girls and they were a rough lot, tough as well. They had more strength than us – we were married women bringing up children. There was one once who winded me – she ran right into me.

Aided by the US War Department's *Instructions for American Servicemen in Britain*, US troops quickly became an integral part of life in Salisbury. This thirty-one-page, pocket-sized book had been written for a body of men for whom Britain would have been their first taste of life outside their homeland – possibly their state. Among its tips on becoming 'more acquainted with the British, their country and their ways' was some rather helpful advice about that great British institution, the pub. 'The British have theaters and movies (which they call 'cinemas') as we do but the great place of recreation is the pub,' the guide said. 'The British are beer drinkers – and can hold it. The beer is now below peacetime strength but can still make a man's tongue wag at both ends.'

Gordon Monger recalls:

World heavyweight boxing champion Joe Louis, whose victory over German Max Schmeling had been broadcast live over the radio from New York City, was among the top talent brought in by the US Army to thrill the locals of Salisbury.

Big band leader Glenn Miller was a hit at Salisbury's Victoria Park.

There were soldiers all around the city all the time and at night the pubs were full of troops, especially when the Americans came – and they didn't like our warm beer.

The streets were in the blackout and the American soldiers were everywhere trying to pick up the girls as you can imagine, and there was honky tonky going on all over the place! It was a lovely time in a way.

Of course, the combination could prove explosive:

I can recall walking up Fisherton Street one night and the airborne division was fighting with the American troops and they lined up on each side of the road to have a go at one another. I can recall several incidents. They used to have to relax and that was how they found their relaxation.

To teenage Ray Elliott, it was all an adventure:

It makes it sound as if the war was fun and it was in a way because you are only young once and you have got to have fun where you can find it, but in later years when you find out what was going on, it was no joke.

Doughnuts were among the treats missing from the rationed domestic diet that GIs would gift to Britons from their supplies.

Bette Blackwell recalls one GI and his dog who were a familiar sight around Salisbury were sadly drowned at sea.

The War Department's guide also spelled out the tough realities of domestic life for the British, compared with life at home back in the US, where provisions remained plentiful. 'If you are invited into a British home and the host exhorts you to: "Eat up there's plenty on the table," go easy,' the book warned. 'It may be the family's rations for a whole week spread out to show their hospitality.'

Such words went a long way, says Gordon:

Us telegraph boys enjoyed the Americans because we always got a good tip. We used to go to the bottom of Wordsworth Road and the trains used to stop along there to go into the tunnel and the soldiers were all looking out and us youngsters were shouting for chocolate and cigarettes and they'd throw them out the window! They were generous, very generous.

Adele Stokes agrees:

They were absolutely wonderful, they loved children: they knew we'd gone without a tremendous amount. Because we couldn't have sweets we'd have to suck a Zubes cough lozenge, or a Fisherman's Friend that used to burn your throat. The troop trains would come up to Salisbury, filled with GIs hanging out the window, and the children would be waiting and they'd throw all these goodies out to the children: chocolate bars, fruit – they were very kind to us.

Joan Johns, at Wellworthy Piston Rings, remembers how soldiers would visit her parents' house bearing such wonderful gifts as sweets and chocolate:

> There were a tremendous lot of Americans and they used to come into Salisbury. They would come and have tea with mum and bring us goodies. The ones we met were rankers [ordinary GIs] ... they were probably farm hands from the Deep South or something. They were ordinary, and lovely people.

Another common gift was tins of fruit, missing from the British meal table. Adele says:

> They used to come to our house and we didn't have hardly anything, but my mother you can imagine she had a big rabbit stew on, and those Yanks loved my mum's rabbit stew and all the fresh vegetables and they were really kind to us and we really cared about them and they were really lovely people.

Bonds were quickly formed in this atmosphere, but they were not always lasting or deep. Roy Fittall was returning from a long walk one evening with his family when his younger sister began to flag. That was when an American serviceman stepped in:

> This chap came up behind and said: 'Come on luv I'll carry you.' He was an American and we only knew him as 'Johnny' but he carried her to our house. He came in for a coffee and a chat. He came in one or two times after that and brought a food parcel – that was all right. Then he came in to say he was going back home, because he'd been wounded – he was a side gunner in a Flying Fortress and he'd received a Purple Heart medal and was sent home. We wrote to him at an address that he gave us, but we received a reply saying not known at that address. We never did know his real name.

Doreen Andrews was five when the war began and lived opposite the Wilts and Dorset on Castle Street that her father would watch over for fires and where her aunty worked on wings. She recalls children like her being invited by the US troops to fantastic parties at the PX:

> The Americans would walk down the street and give you a little note to take to your parents saying they were having a party at what was the PX and, oh, what a feast we had. Nobody came with us – we trusted them – we had sweets and cookies and there was a doughnut-eating competition where we had to eat as many as we could. That was great! That was heaven! That was the biggest treat in the war!

Doreen Andrews remembers parties at the PX with sweets and a doughnut-eating competition. 'We had to eat as many as we could ... That was the biggest treat in the war!'

Dances were a great way for Spitfire workers to let off steam and forget the concerns of war.

Among those swept up one day was Roy:

> I went to Salisbury market to collect my paper round with a friend and this American came up and asked us: 'Do you want to join my army?' Well, we thought him a bit of an idiot, but we said: 'Yes, all right,' and he said: 'Follow me!' So we went with him and it was near Christmas and he took us into Woolworths, which had been turned into the PX. They had a load of kids in there and cakes and tea and everything and we all got given a present – we had a good night.

The Americans seemed dashing, too, in their neat uniforms. Adele recalls the attention she received from one particular officer while working in a china and glassware shop:

> We used to have a major who'd come in – Major Ude – he was charming and looked glamorous in his uniform and he kept coming in for tubes of glue and my boss used to say: 'Why's the major coming for tubes of glue, I'm sure he'd send one of his boys in. He must break an awful lot of china.' And he'd look at me and laugh because Major Ude always made a beeline for me – the blonde one. He'd say: 'Is the blonde one here?' It was just fun you know. And we all used to laugh and say: 'He's broken some more china!' It was all fun, but he was lovely looking and he had a lovely uniform.

The nurses at Odstock's hospital made an impression, too. Adele says:

> They were very attractive in their beautiful gabardine, cream-coloured straight skirts and dark jackets. They wore beautiful hats that were quite high with a peaked cap, and had lovely leather, mid-brown handbags and lace-up shoes with a small heel, and they wore nylon stockings that we didn't have, and they were very charming.

Nylons were something the women of the Spitfire factories could not ordinarily get, so they would attempt to emulate them by colouring their legs light brown and painting a fine line down the length of the back of the leg. 'We'd envy the American girls,' recalls Betty Potter from Trowbridge. 'We had to draw a line up our legs – we never had any nylons.'

Joyce, who Betty worked with, agrees: 'When we saw the nylon stockings! Oh, how we wished we had a pair!'

Inevitably, the war would intrude and remind everybody just how much was at stake. Bette says:

The American soldiers all left us one evening because they said that they had a big job to do the next day – that they were all going to the seaside, but they couldn't tell us where because they didn't know themselves where they were going. The next day we saw some of them and we asked where so-and-so was, and the one that I was friendly with – he didn't come back and he had a little dog that he took everywhere with him. The little dog and him were drowned.

Joan Burrough recalls the aftermath of D-Day, which claimed 4,000 Allied soldiers' lives, including many of those stationed in the Salisbury area:

We were at a dance at the hospital and they called for the ambulance drivers, and they had to drive to Stockbridge. People from the beach were brought back to Southampton on the boats and from there up to Stockbridge on the train and the ambulance had to meet them down there and take them to the hospital. Some had passed away on the journey and were covered in blankets, others had their jackets torn off and were all banged up, and some just managed to wave their hand. It's a sight you won't forget. Straight from the battlefield they were, they were all muddy. It wasn't very nice.

Bad news was part of wartime life but the burden of delivering unwelcome messages to relatives of those killed on the front line fell to Gordon, the telegram boy:

There were many incidents where I had to deliver a telegram that sadly said the husband or the brother had been killed. You rang the bell and you were awfully worked up about it. And they'd come to the door, and the look on their face alone was absolutely shattering. And they'd take the telegram and open it, and I felt almost as bad as they did at that time. Sometimes they'd burst into tears or they'd call out for mothers, brothers – or somebody else in the house. It was an awful job to do.

Adele was on Gordon's route. She had one older brother serving in the RAF as a tail gunner on a bomber, which was a dangerous and unenviable post. Nicknamed tail-end Charlies, they occupied one of the most exposed positions, picked out in a perspex bubble on the tip of the tail serving as observer and gunner in mighty aircraft such as the four-engine Avro Lancaster. His would be one of the easiest positions for an enemy pilot to pick off, while any escape from a damaged or stricken bomber was expected to be made via a tiny hatch at the back of the pod. Being wedged between seat and guns and wearing a bulky flying suit would make escape a near-impossible task. Little wonder Adele would watch anxiously for Gordon, hoping he would walk straight past her mother's house. 'Once he went past my mother's house I knew everything would be alright, but I did worry who he was going to. He was on his way round to somebody, so I was still upset because I knew my mother didn't have a telegram but somebody else was going to get one and be upset,' she says.

The blackout was another inescapable reality that meant shops, homes and businesses such as those turned over to Spitfire production had to douse their lights to the outside world during night-time hours. Street lights, signs and vehicle lights were either removed or hooded. Windows would be blocked using thick curtains,

Adele Stokes protected her younger brothers as a Focke-Wulf bore down on them.

cardboard or paint and it was among the duties of the Air Raid Precautions (ARP) wardens to patrol the streets and ensure the blackout was observed and that not a chink of light escaped. The blackout was meant to help deny German bombers easy markers, even though they were actually directed to their targets using radio signals sent from stations in France. For many like Stan Gordon, at the Witt and Vincent Garage undertaking welding and working on Spitfire tanks, the blackout was a defining experience. 'The other thing I remember about the war principally, apart from rationing, was the blackout – you can't imagine life without any lights. A glimmer here and a glimmer there,' Stan says. 'Handy for courting, mind.' The darkness was absolute. 'You couldn't have a torch – you just had to remember where you were,' Pat Pearce says.

Before being called up to work at Wellworthy Piston Rings, Joan Johns served as an ARP warden with her father and a friend:

> We patrolled in the evenings and at night ... in your spare time you went walking the streets checking for problems and making sure people weren't shining a light. We used to hear the German bombers going over every night and I assumed they were going to bomb Bristol. You could hear these awful engines. They seemed different to every other engine – quite different to a British Lancaster or anything like that.

Others also became practised at identifying German bombers by the sound of the engines. Hilda, recently married and living at Queen Alexandra Road barely a mile from Salisbury's gasworks, remembers nights alone because her police constable husband was out on his patrol:

> I was petrified having never slept alone in a house before. I remember lying in bed literally shaking when I heard the German planes go over in the early hours of the morning. You could tell the German planes because they had a certain drone.

Those bombers might have been heading to Bristol but you never knew when they might unload on the secret Spitfire city, and Adele recalls listening to infamous Nazi propagandist William Joyce, better known as Lord Haw-Haw, on her radio at home, threatening destruction. 'We'd listen to Haw-Haw and once he said: 'It's all right Salisbury, we haven't forgotten you.' And it frightened us – we thought we are going to get it now – they are going to bomb us. We were lucky in a way, in that the blackout saved a lot of our heartache.'

Women's football was popular and Bette Blackwell (far right) played against the Army. 'They were a rough lot, tough as well.'

Milk boy Ken Hayter captures the spirit inside one of the secret factories he visited on an early morning delivery round.

It might have helped save lives but, like many, Hilda was glad to eventually see the back of the blackout when the war ended. 'That was the greatest joy when peace was proclaimed, we ripped down the blackout because we had had so many years of every evening, as soon as it got dark, up went the blackout.' Stanley Jones recalls the thrill of the end of blackout in Trowbridge:

> By today's standards this would be merely a glimmer but to us children it was wonderful – and we were allowed to play outside. I think all the children were out – just dancing around the street lamps. It was not very long before all the local shops had wonderful illuminated displays – it was like fairyland. The dark long nights had gone.[27]

Inside the Spitfire factories, the wartime sweat and toil forged a sense of equality and comradeship. The hours may have been long but Bill Edwards recalls everybody mucking in regardless of background or position in the factory. He sums up the Castle Road factories through the shared experience of break times: 'They had a lovely canteen that catered for 200 people and everybody just went in – it didn't matter if you were a boss or whatever, it was just like a big family and it was really great.'

There was the added bonus of being on the outskirts of Salisbury, in the shadow of the Iron Age hill fort and medieval settlement of Old Sarum where the night-shift workers would enjoy breaks under the stars. Norman Parker says:

> During the summer nights, at lunchtime or for their evening meal, workers would often go up and have a picnic at Old Sarum and at two or three o'clock in the morning come down the road to the works again singing away at the top of their voices, and wake the neighbours up.
>
> It was free and easy, and I mean free and easy in a real positive sense, because as a young lad my education was completed by what I saw going on around the various places.

Breaks were limited in number and Joan Burrough recalls one inventive answer to obtaining that much-needed cuppa at Chattis Hill. 'We had a tea trolley brought round for a cup of tea but somebody in the paint shop had a stove. And I remember a cardboard box being carried up through our factory with steam coming out of it. They'd made a pot of tea and brought it in – for an extra cup of tea,' she says.

There was also time for romance and it was through working on Spitfires that Joan Burrough would find herself smitten by a certain young lad named Ted, who went to work at Chattis Hill following the bombing of Southampton. Supermarine's management were strict on staff socialising during work hours to keep the production lines rolling and hit targets, but they seem to have relaxed the rules for the joint interests of true love and wartime morale. 'It was in the factory where I met him, but working on the other side of the factory to me. I used to slip across there to talk to him and in the end the manager asked if I would like to work with him,' she recalls, laughing.

News of their eventual marriage was picked up by journalists in the area. 'There was an article in the local newspaper: "Fitters mate for life" the headline said, but they thought it might be better for the war effort if we worked together!'

All the while a new generation of boys was growing up, ready to take the controls of the Spitfires that they had little idea were being manufactured behind the everyday facades of local businesses in Salisbury and beyond. Ray was a member of the Air Cadets, busy learning aircraft recognition, navigation and mathematics, inspired by the older boys from his school who'd joined the RAF:

> Shortly after they left school, they had a course in how to fly a Spitfire and they'd come back to school with their flying officers' wings or observer half-wing ... so all of us wanted to be Spitfire pilots. We couldn't wait to get there. So our education had a purpose: we were going to qualify to become Spitfire pilots.

Stan juggled metalwork at Witt and Vincent with ARP work and cadet training. 'My teenage years were very busy: I was here working all day and sometimes overtime, I was in the cadets because I was keen to join the RAF and I was an ARP civil defence manager. My turn came to join the RAF and suddenly the war was over! I was transferred to the Army and ended up in Germany,' says Stan. With hindsight, however, his views changed: 'When I read about air gunners, I was glad I missed it!'

When he wasn't delivering telegrams, Gordon trained with the Air Training Corps (ATC). He says:

> All the boys at school were more excited than worried about the war – it was all an adventure for us. No one had any big worries – everyone wanted to get into the Air Corps to do their bit when they were old enough.
>
> I've still got my book at home called *Aircraft Mathematics*, which is solely about arithmetic for aircraft crew and all the boys in the ATC were hoping to become air crew. The clever ones were pilots and the rest were gunners or navigators. The majority turned out as air crew or engineers.

Supermarine relaxed the rules on fraternisation for Joan Burrough, who met her husband Ted working at Chattis Hill.

For these boys, however, their time would never come. The Spitfires built for the RAF helped turn the tables on the Luftwaffe and ultimately Hitler's military machine, bringing it to its knees before the new recruits would get the chance to clamber aboard a Spitfire for their country. In helping defeat Hitler, the factories didn't simply play a part in shaping the course of the war, they transformed the lives of those working in them – especially the thousands of women thrown into a line of work previously considered 'unsuitable'. Riveting and welding sheet metal and wiring Spitfires, they'd found a kind of calling. Long days and nights spent standing or squeezing into tight spaces, handling heavy equipment and withstanding penetrating cold while working in secret from their families, were offset by workplace camaraderie and adventure. These workers would be relatively handsomely rewarded, earning much more than they could have in other lines of war work. But remuneration wasn't the point for the members of this hidden army.

Contributing to the war effort in a meaningful role by helping to deliver this iconic and lethal aircraft, with colleagues who quickly became friends, would be the reward. 'We had very, very hard days but I think where I worked we all loved our work – we all helped out if anybody was away or if one of the men was transferred to the Army,' says Joyce.

It sums up the workplace, the workers and a union born of building the Spitfire: 'We didn't keep wishing the work would end but we did wish the war would,' she says. 'We enjoyed the work because it was friendly. I suppose we were all working together.'

NOT JUST DIGGING FOR VICTORY

If Britain's indomitable wartime Prime Minister Winston Churchill had a dark fear it was of the country being starved into submission by Hitler. 'The only thing that ever really frightened me during the war was the U-boat peril,'[28] Churchill conceded, years after the Allies' victory. Britain depended significantly on imports from the rest of the world, annually consuming 20 million tonnes of food from overseas including meat from such far-flung places as New Zealand. Hitler therefore planned to sink merchant shipping heading to and from Britain, something he attempted using his Navy's submarines called U-boats, in the waters of the North Atlantic.

With the start of the Battle of the Atlantic in September 1939, the Government set about trying to ensure adequate supplies of at least the staples. It attempted this through a system of rationing that, over time, would allocate a small weekly amount of many items per household based on weight and then points and value. Bacon, butter and sugar were the first to be rationed, in January 1940, with the system progressively extended to other items such as jam and tea. Some produce such as fruit wasn't rationed but simply became more difficult to obtain, with oranges, for example, prioritised for children. Collecting your weekly ration at the butcher, baker or elsewhere involved taking your identity card and ration book, although getting your allocation wasn't a role reserved for adults. Doreen Andrews, who lived opposite the secret Spitfire factory at the Wilts & Dorset Bus Garage on Castle Street, remembers mucking in as a child:

> My mum was quite poorly and I was only 6 or 7 when I did the ration books. I had to do the shopping so I knew how many points we had and what we could have. I used to get meat in the morning and bread after school. It became a way of life.

Flexibility was the key to stretching the meagre weekly rations of staples such as dairy products:

> The rations included a piece of cheese for all of us. My brother liked butter but wouldn't eat margarine, so my brother got the butter because he was the favourite and we got the margarine and dad had the cheese for his sandwich. I don't know how people managed, but we always had a meal on the table.

Adele Stokes, living with her mum and her younger brothers in Salisbury, also participated in the domestic food trading, swapping sugar, which was rationed to 8oz (226.7g) per week, for tea, which was limited to just 2oz [56.6g]. 'My sister-in-law didn't take sugar and I did, so we'd swap a little bit of tea for sugar. There was lots of swapping about,' she says.

With each household getting just one egg a week and an allowance of inferior, dried substitute from the US, these golden wonders were a luxury. Should you come into a few extras, well that was a cause for small celebration, as Adele discovered. 'We had one egg a week but if somebody gave mother a few eggs from their chickens, she would crack one open, mix up the yolk and put it all over my hair to "keep it nice and blonde".'

The white of the egg she whisked up and used as a face mask. She said: 'I'm going to lie down, don't disturb me!' And we dare not – the white of the egg stiffened her skin and she couldn't speak and she couldn't tell us off if we did do anything wrong, so we didn't mind her keeping her face mask on as we got away with a few naughty things.'

Such moments illustrate the dearth of food, with even the humble potato becoming a valued commodity. Adele picks up the story:

I remember when we had very little food, my friend across the road was told to peel the potatoes by her mother. She peeled the potatoes and then her mother came out and said: 'You come back in and peel the rest of the potato off those peelings – you haven't peeled them thin enough. So you just peel them again and I've got more to put on the plates.'

Adele Stokes' father turned to nature to supplement the family rations and bring in extra money, catching rabbits which Adele sold locally.

Potatoes were among the vegetables that the Government encouraged the nation to grow to help supplement meals, rather than wait on supplies from farms or overseas. A month after Britain entered the war, and just ahead of the introduction of rationing, the Minister of Food exhorted Britons to roll up their sleeves and start running their own allotments. 'So let's get going,' Sir Reginald Dorman Smith said in October 1939. 'Let "dig for victory" be the motto of everyone with a garden and every able-bodied man and woman capable of digging an allotment in their spare time.'

Private gardens, public parks, railway embankments and other green spaces went under the plough to such an extent that by 1942 the number of allotments in England and Wales had risen to 1.45 million – up from 815,000 in 1939.[29]

In keeping with the national call, the people of Salisbury dug for victory. Adele recalls how a system developed of growing produce and then recycling leftovers and other bits so that nothing was wasted:

> We had such beautiful vegetables. The fathers all had allotments and all the vegetable peelings – tomatoes, carrots, sprouts – went into big bins and a man came once a week to take the bins away for the pigs. The lady I lodged with put a great big cauldron on the stove full of peelings and it smelt disgusting – that was to feed the pigs.

Hilda Mitchenere had only recently got married and moved into a house near the Salisbury Gas Light and Coke Company with her police constable husband. She remembers: 'There were hard times, but we had quite a large garden at the gas works and one of the men working there would help in the garden and would get repaid with as much fruit and vegetables as he could carry.'

Manure from the horses that pulled wagon loads of coke and coal would be gathered up for use on vegetable beds.

With meat in short supply, people would keep chickens, not only for those highly prized eggs but also for the occasional Sunday lunch once the bird's laying days were over. The Government and local authorities had for many years actively discouraged the keeping of poultry in back-garden runs but that policy went into full reverse during the war, as the authorities exhorted suburbanites to keep chickens and rabbits for food use. Despite becoming a popular form of domestic livestock, a chicken meal remained a relatively rare treat. Hilda recalls fondly: 'We kept chickens, so we did have eggs and the occasional roast chicken, which were absolutely wonderful.'

Rabbits were a different matter and, with Salisbury surrounded by open country and farmland, those who were willing and able to plunder the wild rabbit populations could supplement the meagre meat ration and bulk out their vegetable-centric diet, while also making a little money on the side selling rabbits to the neighbours.

One of those was Adele's dad:

My father used to go rabbiting with his ferrets and I'd help him make the nets and when he came home, he'd say: 'You sell my rabbits,' and I said: 'Why can't the boys, I don't like those rabbits hanging from my finger.' And my father said: 'People don't say no to you but they do to the boys when they try selling them.' He was right: I always went home with the money and they always took the rabbits off me!

Rabbit was on the menu at home, too, going into the stews her mum would cook for the family and the US servicemen stationed in the area who'd pop by for a taste of home cooking. In return the GIs would bring food such as tinned fruit that was easy for them to obtain through army supplies but that had disappeared from the Great British diet thanks to the war in the Atlantic. Adele's guests might have appreciated the stew, less so Adele. 'Rabbit supplemented us a bit,' she recalls, 'but I couldn't eat a rabbit now!'

Joan Johns avoided the worst food privations by being on a farm. 'The farmer's wife used to make the most wonderful rice puddings – they were so creamy.'

One potentially easy way to get that little bit of extra food during the war was to work on a farm, as did tens of thousands of adults and children responding to the Government's call to 'lend a hand on the land'. Many farmers had gone to war, while the square-acreage of farmland had increased to deliver greater self-sufficiency. Of course, what you ate depended on the type of farm. Joan Johns, who worked at Wellworthy Piston Rings that was part of a network of suppliers feeding Spitfire production, was one of those also on the land. 'I was on a farm on the way to Southampton and the farmer's wife used to make the most wonderful rice puddings – they were so creamy. During the war, I can't remember being hungry.'

Children also became part of Salisbury's agricultural labour force, either being taken out of school or simply having to sacrifice part of their holidays to help out at particularly busy times such as harvest. Salisbury lad Ray Elliott was among them:

> Children were expected to go to the market square and a farm lorry would come by and pick you up, and you'd be selected for something like potato picking. We worked our socks off – and it was October, so it was chilly – but it's what we were expected to do.

Doreen was out there, too:

> We'd be picked up in the town and you got two weeks off school – which was very good – and we'd go out on the back of a truck and a nice little man called Pete, wearing a little trilby hat, would drive us out and we'd park up and go into this field. That was damn hard work – it was back-breaking. We had a plot to work over and someone would come round and turn the potatoes up and we had to put them into the sacks and have them ready to be picked up. Then we had to move over to the next lot and we had to be ready.

Local boy Roy Fittall remembers eating relatively well while also making some handy cash by living off and working the land around Salisbury:

> We could go out mushrooming, blackberrying, pinching apples from the farmers' fields. Then a lorry would draw up outside the school and you'd all go out potato picking. That was all right, because you could get four shillings and sixpence a day – that was like a fortune and you didn't mind missing school lessons!

The workload was so great that German and Italian prisoners of war held in the area were drafted in to assist. Doreen says:

We used to take them out to the farms – I remember sitting on one of the prisoner's knees in the front of the truck. We'd take out around fifteen. They were just boys and they had their hats on, with their peaks, and they would make gifts like wooden cigarette cases and ships in bottles. Dad gave them cigarettes in place of these little gifts.

It was a human chapter in the war, with no ill will towards their captured enemies, as Doreen recalls:

I don't think we felt badly about them. I didn't – it was just a natural thing we were doing – we knew Dad had gone to get the prisoners. You can imagine they were going to get some nasty-looking men but they were all boys – about 18 – and some of them never went home. Some stayed and married Salisbury people when they were released.

SALISBURY'S STARS AND STRIPES HOSPITAL

US troops had been stationed in and around Salisbury in huge numbers in preparation for the D-Day landings in northern France. Allied commanders had braced themselves for 40,000 casualties just on the first day of the operation and while, thankfully, they suffered considerably less – a quarter of that number – even that figure, combined with the later casualties as the fighting moved inland, would have overwhelmed Salisbury's existing medical facilities. The city had a hospital – the Salisbury General Infirmary established in 1771 – and while it had served the peacetime needs of the local population, even by ordinary standards it was struggling financially. Construction of a new outpatients wing in 1936 was only made possible through charitable donations – among them from First World War poet Siegfried Sassoon.

Work on a new US hospital in Salisbury therefore began in 1942 at the village of Odstock, about 2.6 miles (4.1km) to the south of the city centre, with British workmen erecting a basic, brick and Nissen hut facility that consisted of twelve buildings with 600 beds. The hospital included two large officers' wards and an isolation ward, pharmacy, laboratories, administration and X-ray facilities. Why Nissen huts? A concept devised during the First World War, Nissen-style construction had become popular with the military as a durable form of enclosed shelter that was quick and simple to erect. Nissen huts are half-cylindrical structures built using a series of corrugated metal sheets fitted together to form a curved roof with walls. Built under wartime conditions, with a stretched British labour force and shortage of materials, it was to prove a little too basic.

It was the US Army 5th General Hospital Unit that inherited this new set-up. One of more than 200 US-based hospitals and medical operations sent abroad by the US War Department by 1943, the 5th General had been

The 158th General Hospital cared for 10,000 patients during its operational lifetime.

A three-month repair and upgrade programme by US Army engineers and medical staff delivered a modern, 1,000-bed facility.

Medics, nurses and patients relocated from the hospital's initial site in Northern Ireland.

Pathology Department 1941

Len   Dr.   Dr.   Dr.
Brown   Dennady   Thornton   Gubbin

Dorothy   Sybil   Ted
Bram   Gage   Searle

The 158th specialised in care of soldiers suffering from combat fatigue.

stationed in Northern Ireland but was relocated to Odstock. An advance party of forty-eight officers and enlisted men arrived in December 1942, followed by 380 more, including nurses, civilian employees, Red Cross staff and the remaining officers and enlisted men. With them came more than 300 patients. What they found was a hospital lacking in heating and electricity and in need of urgent repair thanks to water damage in the living and washing areas caused by a leaking roof. Odstock was also small: with D-Day coming, a hospital almost double the size was envisioned. An urgent repair and upgrade programme was therefore undertaken by US Army engineers and medical staff to deliver a modern, 1,000-bed facility.

Roof repair and fixing water damage were a first priority. The engineers also had to install a suitable source of power of the correct voltage required for US-designed medical equipment, while a gas supply was laid on for the laboratory, pharmacy, central supply and dental buildings. A series of physical improvements included building enclosed walkways between wards and resurfacing roads and walkways. This made it easier and safer both to transport patients in beds around the grounds and to deliver medical, fuel and other supplies and remove waste. They achieved all this in just three months and the final walls were painted in time for the hospital to officially open for business in March 1943.

The 5th General Hospital was renamed the 158th General Hospital and during its operational lifetime cared for around 10,000 patients. It specialised in treating soldiers suffering from combat fatigue – also known as shell shock or nowadays Post Traumatic Stress Disorder (PTSD) – a form of anxiety-related neurotic disorder brought on by exposure to battle. More than just a hospital, it organised entertainment, too, with dances and events designed to speed the recovery of patients, boost the morale of locals and help US troops integrate with the community.

At the end of the war, Odstock was handed over by the US military to become part of the fledgling National Health Service, created in 1948. Over the decades the hospital has changed and expanded, the Nissen huts now long gone, and Salisbury Hospital has become part of the Salisbury NHS Foundation Trust serving 240,000 people annually in Wiltshire, Dorset and Hampshire. The number of beds has halved but the staff has grown to more than 4,000 as the hospital has expanded to offer more services, including specialised work on burns, plastic surgery and spinal rehabilitation.

THE RADIO DAYS THAT SHAPED A NATION

Radio was a ubiquitous presence in the working and domestic lives of wartime Britons, including those in and around Supermarine's hidden Spitfire factories. Whether clustered around a radio set during the blackout or listening to a programme on the factory floor, radio became the nation's main form of news and entertainment. The British Broadcasting Corporation (BBC) operated a near monopoly at this time and audiences for its radio programmes were measured in the millions. Still more tuned in overseas, in occupied Europe and the Third Reich where the Gestapo[30] estimated 10–15 million were breaking the law by tuning into the BBC by 1944.

The BBC built on the platform's power to connect directly to listeners – but not before the existing inter-war service had been overhauled to flush out its stuffier elements. That resulted in the BBC Home Service and Forces Network with live concerts, broadcasts from factories, request programmes with the likes of Vera Lynn and children's programming. Doreen Andrews lived in Castle Street opposite the Wilts and Dorset Bus Garage that had been converted into a covert factory turning out Spitfire wings. Oblivious to the factory's purpose, one of young Doreen's recollections is of the music from such programmes drifting out from inside.

The BBC's new formats turned programmes and presenters into national institutions and characters and catchphrases into staples. Among these programmes was *ITMA* (It's That Man Again) whose episodes revolved around frivolous plotlines involving characters such as Mrs Mopp and drew a peak weekly audience of 16 million. It was *ITMA*'s catchphrases that proved the BBC had really struck gold, with 'I'm going down now'[31] uttered by more than one RAF pilot over the radio as they went in to attack the enemy. *The Kitchen Front* was another hit, regularly pulling in a listenership of 14 million housewives with official advice on food and wartime diet, while the *The Brains Trust*, a discussion with leading thinkers of the day, hit 10 million. The speeches of Prime Minister Winston Churchill were broadcast along with those of King George VI at important times, such as Christmas. The King's speech became part of the festive routine, according to Stanley Jones, a boy at the time in Trowbridge. 'The most important thing was that all the Christmas dinner's pots, pans and dishes had to be washed up before the King on the radio,' Stanley remembers.[32]

More than just programming, the BBC delivered certainty in uncertain times. To help ensure continuous broadcasts, the BBC had introduced a network of sixty-one low-powered transmitters around the country all on the same frequency. Should one or more transmitters serving an area be destroyed or forced to close down during a raid, listeners could continue to receive the same programme from another transmitter – albeit with a slightly weaker signal. Shut down could be ordered ahead of an approaching raid as the Luftwaffe's bombers could use transmissions in a system of radio wave-based direction finding.

A network of 213 national radio relay companies also operated across the country that – for a fee – could broadcast signals to a speaker installed at your home via a fixed cable, thereby further sidestepping transmitters. News presenters held the nation's attention, staying at their microphones at the corporation's head office in Broadcasting House, central London, as the Luftwaffe's bombs rained down outside. Journalists risked their lives from war zones, too. Broadcasting legend Richard Dimbleby broke new ground in January 1943 by accompanying an RAF crew on a bombing raid over Berlin. This was a long way from the pre-war BBC, whose newsreaders dressed in formal suits – something that persisted until the outbreak of war in 1939. Something else also changed: the accent bar of using only presenters drawn from the South-East and possessing what the corporation considered to have the 'right' pronunciation was breached with the introduction of Yorkshire actor Wilfred Pickles as a news reporter.

Such commitment and service made an impression on even the youngest of minds. Stanley says:

> We owe such a lot to them. There were many stories of their bravery that didn't come out until after the end of the war. Then there were the reporters – Richard Dimbleby, Frank Gillard, Wynford Vaughan-Thomas to mention just three – who brought us reports from high over Germany in bombers or with the troops on the front line. As the war went on I understood more of what was going on, so I listened to the reports of these men with increased interest.[33]

Miles away in Salisbury, a young Ray Elliott hung on the BBC's words: 'They just told us what was going on and what we were doing. And they would reassure us, saying: "It will be hard but don't worry we will get there."'

The spread and influence of this medium meant that wartime propaganda became synonymous with radio. The dictatorships in Germany, Italy and Japan believed in radio's power to educate and terrify the masses, to move the national spirit. German propaganda minister Joseph Goebbels called radio the 'eighth great power' and the Nazis subsidised the creation of a People's Radio that would help disseminate propaganda.

The BBC didn't engage in such crude and co-ordinated official propagandising. Neither the BBC nor the Government saw a need to flood the nation with affordable radio sets. There might be a war on, but Britons still had to buy their own sets – electronics housed in chunky wooden cases – and pay the BBC licence fee to use them. The BBC was, however, censored and it did follow Government rules on what could be broadcast. Officials vetted scripts to ensure details such as regiment names and positions and details about troop numbers were not revealed. Ray's parents used what they could to chart the war's progress. 'We had a big coloured map on the wall in the kitchen that would show you the front line,' Ray says. 'I'd follow the progress of the war using pins.'

The BBC also ran stirring features and commentary: among them *Spitfires over Britain*, 'the story of the life and work of the men who fly Britain's planes', according to the *Radio Times* of the day.

The BBC might have enjoyed an almost total monopoly on British broadcasting but it didn't entirely control the nation's ears. The arrival of US troops brought the American Forces Network to Britain from July 1943 and that meant more comedy plus – critically – something the BBC's directors would never countenance: swing music. Swing swept the nation's dance halls, fuelled by the popularity of big band leader Glenn Miller and with dance routines such as the Jitterbug setting dance floors alight. Sadly for Britons, and fortunately for the BBC, American Forces Network offered relatively limited competition: broadcasting on low-power transmitters meant its radio signals could not travel far, so it was available mostly only in the vicinity of US bases and it didn't make it to London. Just one in ten Britons[34] could pick up the sound of the American Forces.

Somebody who proved easier to hear was German propagandist William Joyce, better known as Lord Haw-Haw. An American Briton, Joyce broadcast from Berlin in an attempt by the Nazis to undermine the national spirit and sow fear and doubt. Joyce would spread rumours about sabotage and drop hints that where you lived was next on the Luftwaffe's target list. Up to 6 million[35] Britons were thought to regularly listen to Haw-Haw at the start of the war but numbers later fell. Among those tuned in were newly-wed Joyce Hunt and Joan Little, who worked together on secret Spitfires at Trowbridge. Joyce's husband had been captured by the Germans and was a prisoner of war. Haw-Haw would read out prisoners' names, making him essential listening. 'He'd give three or four names of prisoners of war and every day I used to listen, at 11 o'clock at night,' Joyce recalls. Joan sums up their attitude. 'We never knew what was coming from day to day, what was going to happen, but you had to take it in your stride.'

Ultimately, the reach and influence of Germany's propagandist was limited and in Britain, occupied Europe and even Germany, it was the BBC that connected with people. The BBC had, according to Haw-Haw's boss Goebbels, succeeded in winning the 'intellectual invasion of Europe'.

THE PEOPLE OF SECRET SPITFIRES

Factory Workers

Joan Little (twin sister to Betty Potter)
Hilperton Road
Trowbridge

Betty Potter (twin sister to Joan Little)
Hilperton Road
Trowbridge

Joyce Hunt
Hilperton Road
Trowbridge

Stan Gordon
Witt and Vincent Garage
Salisbury

Joan Burrough
Chattis Hill
Salisbury

Joan Johns
Wellworthy Piston Rings
Salisbury

Bette Blackwell
Wessex Motors
Salisbury

Pat Pearce
Wilts and Dorset Bus Garage
Salisbury

Bill Edwards
Castle Road
Salisbury

Stella Rutter
Hursley Park

Gordon Monger
Worthy Down

Norman Parker
High Post

Residents

Peter Smith
Reading

Hilda Mitchenere
Salisbury

Ray Elliott
Salisbury

Gordon Topp
Salisbury

Doreen Andrews
Salisbury

Roy Fittall
Salisbury

Adele Stokes
Salisbury

John Bletsoe
Salisbury

ATA

Joy Lofthouse

Mary Wilkins-Ellis

NORMAN PARKER: FROM BARNARDO'S BOY TO SPITFIRE HISTORIAN

BY NORMAN PARKER

I was a wartime evacuee and on a long bus journey to start a new life when it hit me what I wanted to do. I had just caught a glimpse of a flight of Wellington bombers outside Mildenhall aerodrome in Suffolk, and while most boys would have leapt at the prospect of becoming a pilot, I wanted something different: to be an engineer. 'I wouldn't mind working on those,' I thought to myself, as the bus left the airfield behind.

Little did I realise what a significant moment that was: six months later I was working on Wellingtons at Vickers-Armstrongs and had begun a journey towards my lifelong association with Spitfires. I became an insider in the remarkable story of the stealth Spitfire factories hidden in the Salisbury area and an historical advisor on *Secret Spitfires*. Not that my formal education would have got me this far: it was fate and an inspired decision that meant I would have first-hand technical experience of this most special of aircraft.

I was born in Balham, London, in March 1926, but circumstances saw that, at the age of 11, I was sent with my brother to Dr Barnardo's at Woodford Bridge, Essex, while my sister went to a nearby girls' home. The Boys' Garden City where I went was a series of twenty modern houses built in the grounds of the former Gwynne

Three years at Barnardo's followed by technical school helped turn a boy with a broken education into a skilled aircraft engineer.

House, with thirty-five boys in each unit and with two adults in charge – we were in Canon Fleming House with a matron and deputy to supervise. We boys did all the housework – cleaning, bed-making – but with one bath for thirty-five boys, bath night was a bit of a problem! All our meals were taken in a large hall with kitchens attached. There were twenty sets of long tables with forms for seating, with matron dishing up food from large cauldrons on aluminium plates and bowls, eaten using steel cutlery – imagine the noise!

Although I settled into this routine quite nicely my education had suffered. Before Barnardo's, I'd already moved from one school to another following my father who had, like so many during that time, been forced to chase work. At 11 I sat an exam for scholarship at a grammar school but failed because, the headmaster said, I'd moved around so much and I hadn't had the opportunity to consolidate what I'd learned. Had I been able to do that, the teacher felt, there was no doubt I'd have got into the grammar school. War was brewing, however, and events would begin to take me in the direction of the Spitfire with evacuation. Barnardo's had a major problem in the form of some 2,000 children living in the London area who had to be moved in case the capital was bombed. How we were all distributed I have no idea, but of the thirty-five boys in our house, twenty – including me – were taken to the village of Fornham St Martin, 2 miles (3.2km) north of Bury St Edmunds in Suffolk, and settled in Fornham House. We lived in what was the children's floor of the manor house with a dining hall in a large garage away from the building with a two-burner oil stove for all cooking.

The winter of 1939/40 was one of the worst on record, but we managed. Again we all mucked in, with everybody assigned jobs and taking part in cooking: it was my job to cut everybody's bread – forty rounds for breakfast and at tea time. However, I also took on another role, one that hinted at my future calling. There was a 'house-boy' aged around 16 or 17 who acted as handyman and whose job it was to look after the home's power plant, a Ruston Hornsby oil engine driving a generator. He was a bit of a lazy type, so he left it to me. That meant that, by the age of 13½, I was running a generating station that entailed checking all the batteries for charge.

Again, I settled into a comfortable domestic existence but, once more, events intervened. At the age of 14, I had to leave for the William Baker Technical School in Hertford, a residential establishment, to train for the adult world of work. I chose to pursue engineering – and it was the best decision I ever made. It was on the journey from Fornham St Martin to Hertford that I had my long-distance encounter with the Mildenhall Wellingtons that sealed my fate. New jobs would be posted at the technical school and one day a position happened to come up at Vickers-Armstrongs in Weybridge, Surrey, building Wellington bombers. 'Right,' I said. 'That's the job for me.'

An inspired choice of career led Norman to High Post and the beginning of a lifelong involvement with secret Spitfires.

I spent a couple of years in the factory installing gun turrets on production aircraft but in the middle of 1942 I joined the service department – a mobile unit that repaired RAF aircraft. Repair was cheaper and quicker than building new, so we had an important role to play and our work had priority. If you wanted a gun turret and there wasn't one available you could request one from an existing aeroplane. In this job, you might be sent to a bomber that had crash-landed in the middle of a field – we often did that. If it was repairable, we'd do that. We'd go out in parties of ten or so, do an assessment of what was required, order a new bomb beam, replacement castings for the undercarriage, new wings ... There was no welding – they were all bolted or riveted parts. We'd jack the plane up, strip out the old undercarriage, repair the engines, replace the bomb beam. Quite often we had to wash blood out of the gun turret where the gunner had been shot – but you just got on and did it. If the bomber was in a field, somebody would chop down trees, fill ditches and the RAF would then come in and take the plane away.

By 1944 the Wellington was being replaced by heavy bombers and I finally got my introduction to the Spitfire in August that year. Around thirty of us were asked to transfer to Vickers Supermarine's service department, which was short of people.

It was here that my interest in this remarkable aircraft began – an interest that would see me work on the *Secret Spitfires* film and book. I was with the service team that travelled around the country, gaining vital first-hand experience of the engineering and build of the Spitfire and the story behind its development. I remember my first posting was to Lee-on-Solent working on the Royal Navy's variant, the Seafire, stripping out optical gunsights and installing gyro sights. I worked on a Spitfire modification programme, too, at Middle Wallop, near Salisbury, adding Vokes air filters. One day I had to put an intercooler into the cooling system on the photographic reconnaissance Spitfire. I remember a lorry turned up with thirty of these and bits and pieces of pipe, and we were briefly told what goes where. The lorry disappeared and we worked out what was required and we just got on with it – no manuals or pictures. It was during this time that I also worked on secret Spitfires at High Post airfield.

Towards the end of the war, I was at RAF Colerne, near Bath, working on Spitfires, helping to bring existing planes up to current RAF standard issue. Some airframes would have been in storage for a while and needed design modifications and mechanical attachments that had been issued after their production. Well, then the war finished and that meant no need for such modifications as there was a glut of Spitfires, so we were all made redundant overnight. I reapplied to Supermarine at High Post, working on servicing experimental aircraft, but people like me who'd been on reserved occupations were dragged into the services. I spent the first three months square bashing and learning to be an airman. I remained in the Salisbury area, meeting my wife and joining the Ministry of Defence at Boscombe Down in 1951, where I stayed for many years.

My years at Vickers served me well: luck and a well-timed career decision meant I would eventually gain hands-on experience of one of history's most remarkable fighting machines. The Spitfire had such a complicated and interesting history that I decided to investigate further after the war, when at least the records were more plentiful, and this research has been with me ever since.

I have been telling the story for the past sixty-five years or so, culminating in becoming an historical advisor to the *Secret Spitfires* project, helping to make that information accessible for all. I have attempted to record key details that could have been lost forever, thanks to the veil of secrecy that surrounded Supermarine's unique Spitfire dispersal programme.

SECRET SPITFIRES' NEXT CHAPTER

A memorial stone was commissioned by Salisbury Cathedral following the release of the *Secret Spitfires* documentary in recognition of the contribution made to the Second World War by those involved. A Secret Spitfires Memorial Trust has also been established by the Salisbury Rugby Club, whose goal is to build a permanent factory monument. Spitfire historian and former Supermarine engineer Norman Parker and RAF Air Marshal Sue Gray, seen here with the Cathedral's memorial stone, marked the Trust's launch on 15 October 2019.

RAF Air Marshal Sue Gray with Norman Parker.

News

PAUL JACOBS/PICTURE EXCLUSIVE, MEDIADRS

The replica Spitfire statue has gone or permanent display Salisbury, where secretive teams, le helped to construc parts for the aircra

Spitfire tribute for secret civilians who built planes in sheds

A lifesized replica Spitfire honouring the civilians who secretly built the fighter planes in sheds and garages during the Second World War has been unveiled near a former factory (Will Humphries writes).

More than 2,000 Spitfires were built in secret in Salisbury after production facilities in Southampton were bombed during the Battle of Britain.

Unqualified girls, boys, women, elderly men and a few engineers worked on the operation, in which industrialised warfare became a cottage industry. Spitfire parts were made in sheds, garages, bus depots, a hotel and even a spare bedroom. Salisbury

was the main site, building 10 per cent of the total during the war, but Spitfires were also made in Reading and Trowbridge.

The replica, which cost £100,000 and stands 20ft high, has gone on permanent display next to Salisbury Rugby Club, one of the secret Spitfire production sites, after a year in storage because of the pandemic.

Chris Whalley, chairman of the Secret Spitfires charity, said that the moment was "very important " for the city and "very emotional, very proud" for him. "We've been working at it for the past three years and Salisbury has had a pretty tough time, with one thing and another," he said.

Those who took part in the operation were

sworn to secrecy and it became wider public knowledge only after the release of the 2016 film *The Secret Spitfires*.

Norman Parker, 95,

an engineer who worked on the planes, said about 40 Spitfires a month were built in Salisbury at one point but the people involved kept their

secret well. "We had one case, there was a couple at a dinner party in the 1970s, and over the dinner table the wife said, 'Oh, I was building Spitfires

in Salisbury' and her husband said, 'No yo weren't, I was'. And i transpired they had both been working i the same factory an didn't know."

(*The Times*/News Licensing)

ABOUT THE AUTHORS

Karl Howman and Ethem Cetintas

Karl Howman and Ethem Cetintas have collaborated for twenty years as Howman & Cetintas, combining their experience in investigative journalism, theatre, film, radio, advertising and documentary making. They wish to thank The History Press and Gavin Clarke for collaborating on their first foray into publishing.

Gavin Clarke

Secret Spitfires was a dream come true for Gavin, an Airfix-generation kid. A writer with more than twenty years' experience, Gavin advises on industrial, innovation and conflict heritage.

The authors wish to thank historian Norman Parker, without whom this book would not have been possible. His research and unfailing help and love for the subject inspired us all.

The authors would also like to thank freelance editorial contributor Sarah Vaux.

CREDITS AND CONTRIBUTORS

Joan Burrough
Joan Johns
Bette Blackwell
Pat Pearce
Bill Edwards
Stella Rutter
Gordon Monger
Peter Smith
Hilda Mitchenere

Ray Elliott
Gordon Topp
Doreen Andrews
Roy Fittall
Adele Stokes
Joy Lofthouse
Mary Wilkins-Ellis
John Bletsoe
Joyce Kolk

Selected Bibliography:

Ray Haas, *Touching the Face of God*, High Flight Productions, 2014.

David Jacobs, *Where Are They Now?*, BBC TV, 1979.

Richard Hillary, *The Last Enemy*, Vintage Books, 2010.

Adolf Galland, *The First and the Last*, Blurb, 2019.

Norman Longmate, *How We Lived Then*, Arrow Books, 1988.

Alfred Price, *Spitfire: A Documentary History*, Macdonald and Jane's, 1977.

Norman Ferguson, *The Battle of Britain: A Miscellany*, Summersdale Publishers, 2015.

Robin Prior, *When Britain Saved the West*, Yale University Press, 2015.

Irene Pilson, *More Memories of Bitterne*, Irene Pilson, 1988.

Angus Calder, *The People's War, Britain 1939–1945*, Pimlico, 1992.

Jeffrey Quill, *Spitfire: A Test Pilot's Story*, Crecy Publishing Ltd, 2012.

Stanley Hooker, *Not Much of an Engineer*, Airlife Publishing, 2005.

Peter Pugh, *The Magic of a Name: The Rolls-Royce Story, Part 1: The First Forty Years*, Icon Books, 2000.

David Isby, *The Decisive Duel*, Abacus, 2012.

Winston Churchill, *Their Finest Hour*, Cassell, 1949.

Stephanie Seul, 'British radio propaganda against Nazi Germany during the Second World War', PhD diss., Faculty of History, University of Cambridge, 1995.

NOTES

Introduction: Building a Legend

1. David Jacobs, *Where Are They Now?*, BBC TV, 1979.
2. Richard Hillary, *The Last Enemy*, Vintage Books, 2010, p.58.
3. James Holland interviews Geoffrey Wellum, 2001.
4. Adolf Galland, *The First and the Last*, Blurb, 2019, p.22.
5. Winston Churchill, House of Commons, Hansard 5th Series Volume 364, 1167, 20 August 1940.
6. Norman Longmate, *How We Lived Then*, Arrow Books, 1988, p.337.

John Gillespie Magee Jr: A Remarkable Life

7. Ray Haas, *Touching the Face of God*, p.152.
8. *Ibid.*, p.162.
9. *Ibid.*, p.159.

Engineering and Design that Made the Spitfire Special

10. Alfred Price, *Spitfire: A Documentary History*, Macdonald and Jane's, 1977, p.32.

Chapter 1: The Road to Dispersal

11. Norman Ferguson, *The Battle of Britain: A Miscellany*, Summersdale Publishers, 2015, p.89.
12. Robin Prior, *When Britain Saved the West*, Yale University Press, 2015, p.232.

We Saw it Burn: Testimony from Inside the Firestorm

13. Irene Pilson, *More Memories of Bitterne*, Irene Pilson, 1988, p.288.
14. Angus Calder, *The People's War, Britain 1939–1945*, Pimlico, 1992, p.217.
15. *Ibid.*

Secret Saviour of the Spitfire

16. Jeffrey Quill, *Spitfire: A Test Pilot's Story*, Crecy Publishing Ltd, 2012, p.144.

Chapter 2: People and Places of the Secret Factories

This Island Salisbury: War Comes to the City

17. 'Our Military History', *OurWilton.org*, www.ourwilton.org/what-we-do/our-military-history.

Chapter 3: Day in the Life of a Factory

18. Courtesy Trowbridge Museum.

Uncle Sam's Rolls-Royce Engines

19. Stanley Hooker, *Not Much of an Engineer*, Airlife Publishing, 2005, p.59.
20. Peter Pugh, *The Magic of a Name: The Rolls-Royce Story, Part 1: The First Forty Years*, Icon Books, 2000, p.234.
21. *Ibid.*, pp.227, 235.

Chapter 4:Take it Away:
Test Pilots, Danger and the ATA

Life on the Edge: The Test Pilots' Story

22. David Isby, *The Decisive Duel*, Abacus, 2012, p.48.
23. Jeffrey Quill, *Spitfire: A Test Pilot's Story*, p.192.
24. *Ibid.*, p.193.
25. *Ibid.*, p.86.

Chapter 5: Clocking Off:
Life Outside the Factory Shift

26. Courtesy Trowbridge Museum.
27. Courtesy Trowbridge Museum.

Not Just Digging for Victory

28. Winston Churchill, *Their Finest Hour*, Cassell, 1949, pp.528–29.
29. Norman Longmate, *How We Lived Then*, p.229.

The Radio Days that Shaped a Nation

30. Stephanie Seul, 'British radio propaganda against Nazi Germany during the Second World War', PhD diss., Faculty of History, University of Cambridge, 1995, pp. 86–87.
31. Angus Calder, *The People's War*, p.362.
32. Courtesy Trowbridge Museum.
33. Courtesy Trowbridge Museum.
34. Angus Calder, *The People's War*, p.362.
35. *Ibid.*, p.65.

In remembrance of our dear friend Ethem Cetintas
1953–2021